Remembering
HERACLITUS

Remembering
HERACLITUS

BY

RICHARD G. GELDARD

LINDISFARNE BOOKS

Published by LINDISFARNE BOOKS
www.lindisfarne.org

ISBN 0-940262-98-3

Library of Congress Cataloging-in-Publication Data

Geldard, Richard G., 1935 –
    Remembering Heraclitus / Richard G. Geldard.
        p. cm.
    Includes bibliographical references.
        1. Heraclitus, of Ephesus   1. Title
    B223.G39 2000
    182'.4—dc21   00-020479

Book Design by STUDIO 31

10 9 8 7 6 5 4 3 2 1

Printed in the United States of America

TABLE OF CONTENTS

ACKNOWLEDGMENTS

My interest in the extant fragments of the writings of Heraclitus began during graduate studies at Stanford University in work with my dissertation advisor, T .B. L. Webster. His sensitivity to the Greek language and the challenges of adequate translation further developed an interest in Greek philosophy first stimulated by the work of William Arrowsmith, with whom I studied Greek tragic drama at the Bread Loaf School of English several years before.

At Bread Loaf, while participating in a production of Arrowsmith's translation of the *Heracles* by Euripides, it became apparent to Arrowsmith that his published translation, then part of the University of Chicago Press *Complete Greek Tragedies*, failed to capture what he termed the *turbulence* of the Greek cultural experience of the fifth century B.C. His radical revisions of the text for this compelling production illustrated the complexities of rendering into English the richness of the Greek experience, especially in crisis, and of such crucial Greek words as *nomos, physis,* and *logos*.

Subsequent summer study at Oxford University on the neglected translations of the Platonist Thomas Taylor, whose work was firmly rejected by later scholars, affirmed for me the overwhelming bias brought on by the Aristotelian hegemony in modern classical scholarship, an example of which was the oft-revised work by Jowett on the dialogues of Plato. From late Jowett editions on into the mid-twentieth century, the natural vitality and metaphysical currents of much of Greek literature, poetry, and philosophy had been stripped of their natural turbulence in favor of logical syntax, clarity of sequence, and mere surface coherence. It was not until the 1960s that greater attention was finally paid to ideas in Greek literature and to the challenges of Greek translation. Much of the credit for creative translation goes to Arrowsmith and his editions of Aristophanes' plays published in that decade.

The effect of translation prior to that fresh impulse had often been to remove the kind of natural ambiguity inherent in the Greek language. Where the English language is generally intolerant of ambiguous reference, the Greek language thrives on it. Heraclitus, in particular, took advantage of such ambiguity, indeed defined reality through its use.

This brief book, falling short as it often does, is nonetheless aimed at a fuller appreciation of the wonderful turbulence of wrestling with the ghost of Heraclitus. The mistakes in the text are mine alone and certainly should not reflect on any earlier influence, particularly the monumental works of Webster and Arrowsmith, in whose spirit I have tried to keep faith.

PREFATORY NOTE ON REMEMBERING

The title of this brief study intends a play on the word *remembering*. The Greek word *anamnesis* means remembering or recollection and is the basis of Plato's theory of knowledge and wisdom. Contrary to John Locke's *tabula rasa* and even to the contemporary science of mind, ancient teachings from many cultures, particularly those which emerged in sacred texts in the crucial period around 500 B.C., begin with the understanding that human beings are born possessing the memory of the divine ground to which they promise one day to return, needing only to remember what has been forgotten in the process of coming into earthly existence. *Anamnesis* suggests also a play on *re-membering*, as in a re-membering, or assembling again the fragments remaining of the work of Heraclitus into a whole frame or the whole man.

The fragments that remain to us may well be the bleached bones of a book entitled *On Nature*, which Heraclitus would have deposited in the precincts of the famed Temple of Artemis in Ephesus, as was the custom. We have something left of this book only because other writers, historians, and philosophers picked up a fragment or two from the dust of archaic Ephesus to make part of their own vision. In some cases, the fragments are treated as jokes or examples of the early naiveté of the Presocratic thinkers. In others, a proper respect renders them useful for our purposes.

If the skeleton of a human being consists of approximately two hundred bones, then what we have of Heraclitus doesn't quite make a whole. Scholars have put together probably sixty legitimate or what I have called essential fragments and seventy or so more dubious ones, and if we flesh them out, as it were, we have enough for a good paleontologist to project a likely looking person, but not enough for an accurate portrait. A weak analogy, to be sure, yet it may make its point. It is the case that the fragments remaining of a manuscript which may or may not have been entitled *On Nature*, plus the doubtful details of a biography, do not a person or a coherent philosophy make. The gaps are great, perhaps too great. And yet — and here is the point — the fragments attributed to Heraclitus by the dozens of sources from Plato onward into late Roman times are sufficiently distinctive that a remarkable portrait does emerge of a brilliant, irascible intellect and seer whose poetic language still attracts our attention and devotion. Even in fragmentary form, his teaching remains essential to a genuine understanding of the human relationship to a reality beyond sensory, or materialist, perceptions.

Another theme suggested by the word *remembering* is its relation to the Greek word for truth, *aletheia*, one translation for which is "not-forgetting," and another is "to uncover." If the truth means not to forget, then searching for the truth involves remembering or uncovering what was previously lost. *Aletheia* was the first word associated with those who practiced philosophy. These were human beings who remembered, who spoke of things forgotten. Later, when this term became too imposing for any one person to assume for the community, these rememberers, or truth-tellers, became *philia-sophos,* lovers of wisdom, a much easier, pleasing sounding activity and an occupation less likely to end in banishment.

Many of the fragments left to us from the work of Heraclitus relate to the act of remembering. It is safe to assume, therefore, that much of *On Nature* also related to that same theme, since it is logical that the fragments reflected the whole work and not just a section of it relating to not-forgetting. Plato's concept of reminiscence gives to the human soul the storehouse of memory to which the conscious human being has access if rightly aligned to receive it. We have to be out there, however, out on the edge of the abyss at midnight, waiting for the word. We are Hamlet on the parapet, hearing the ghost say, "Remember me . . . ."

Finally, for the reader interested in a brief account of the problems of translation, selection and ordering of the fragments, I have provided an appendix, which follows the main text on page 151.

INTRODUCTION

Heraclitus was in his prime, we are told, in 500 B.C., just before what historical tradition calls the Golden Age of Greece, a period which has come to reflect popular notions of culture and politics for Western civilization. Sometime twenty years or so prior to that, still comfortably during what we now call the Archaic Period, Heraclitus chose to walk away from the responsibilities of being a leading member of the ruling family in Ephesus, then a powerful city-state in Asia Minor. Evidently, he preferred a life of study, and in particular, intellectual inquiry into the laws of nature. Even this latter phrase does not quite capture the essence of how and why Heraclitus spent his time as he did. **I searched my nature**, he said, no doubt in answer to someone who asked him, "How do you know what you know?"

To be a philosopher in the time of Heraclitus was to be an instigator as well as an investigator. At the close of what we call the Archaic Period, a time characterized by the dominance of religious myth, a critical shift was taking place throughout the civilized world. A new freedom of intellectual inquiry in particular areas like Ephesus and Miletus permitted those thinkers who possessed the courage and the intelligence to explore alternative explanations for the presence of the world, for human intelligence, for social and economic order, and for the role of divinity in human life. In general we refer to those individuals (including Heraclitus) as investigators, or Natural Philosophers. Looking back, we know what we mean by this term, but of course in 500 B.C. no one would have understood it. As the philosopher Ortega y Gasset noted, the best term for such thinkers at the time was "truth-teller," but as a pastime (before becoming a business) it was dangerous because those who heard these truths and disagreed with the findings often disposed of the teller of the truths. It was therefore much healthier to be known as a Lover of Wisdom, or a philosopher.

The primary function of philosophers was to be investigators, and it has always been assumed that this was their primary function. In the case of the natural philosophers, their role was to examine the natural order in great detail — earth, sea, and sky — in an effort to explain "naturally" what caused and what maintained the existing order. That the thunder was not the wrath of a god was gradually being accepted as fundamental to a new understanding of the cosmos, so when Heraclitus says, **The Lightning directs all things,** he was penetrating beyond myth into the causal realm of nature, and yet he was still employing the language of myth in his explanations of reality.

Geniuses like Heraclitus have always pushed against their received traditions. They are always ahead of the knowledge curve. It may be supposed, wrongly I believe, that the extant fragments of Heraclitus merely address the errors of traditional belief in an attempt to enlighten the ignorant of the basic laws of nature. It is the thesis of this book, however, that Heraclitus was not merely interested in communicating new facts to a population immersed in an outmoded mythological belief system. The fragments reveal much more than a scientific concern for expunging from the minds of ordinary people false notions about superficial nature.

Rather, Heraclitus was fundamentally an instigator, and it was out of this crucial role that his work, of which the fragments are the significant remains, emerged. An instigator is one whose mission is to prod sleeping minds to the waking state, to elevate minds to a higher level of consciousness. In the ancient world, Socrates was the most famous instigator, the gad-fly of classical Athenian society, prodding the sleeping citizens to awaken, to realize who they were and what they must do to preserve their crumbling society. His death was the ultimate sacrifice in this process of instigation. He taught us how to die well, but his real intention was to teach us how to live wisely. In terms of the Athenians, he did not succeed, except in the case of the very few, including his pupil Plato.

Heraclitus was the instigator of archaic Ephesus, which in his time was a powerful city-state devoted to the cult of the goddess Artemis. Ephesus was the most famous site of the goddess, and her temple was one of the Seven Wonders of the World. Ephesus had its beginnings in Neolithic times, eventually became a Mycenean settlement, and then evolved slowly as a major trading center with ties to the Orient and to the Western and Southern Mediterranean. In its prime, the famed harbor of Ephesus extended right up to the foundations of the Temple of Artemis, with the busy, gleaming city within sight of the laden ships. The Cayster River flowed into the harbor and where the fresh water from the mountains merged with the sea, the mixing of the waters became a place sacred to the goddess. It was at this auspicious blending of fresh and salt waters that life-giving powers were concentrated, a fact which modern evolutionary science now confirms. Over the millennia, however, the harbor silted up and gradually, even after major Roman efforts to dredge the harbor back to the temple foundations, the ancient city lost its trading resources and became, literally, a backwater. Today, the temple ruins sit in marsh waters and a lone column marks the center of its former glory.

The mythopoetic influence of the Great Mother Goddess was pervasive even in the rich multi-cultural mix of Ephesean culture. By the Classical period, Artemis was still dominant and was worshiped as goddess of the Moon, and her cult was celebrated in her own festival in the month of Munychion (April-May). This strong feminine influence is important to Heraclitus because rather than the masculine sky gods being dominant as they were in Attic Greek religion and culture, the Ephesian religious ethos always had a strong feminine influence and would have been a strong influence in his vision. As we shall see, rather than the idea of "soul" being a weak, feminine characteristic compared to masculine "spirit" in later Western philosophy and religion, soul for Heraclitus was powerful and possessed both generative and transformative powers.

From the sixth century B.C. on, until well into the Roman era, for roughly a thousand years, Ephesus remained an intellectual and cultural center, as evidenced by the current remains of the great Celsus Library. Its fame rested not only on the magnificence of its temple precinct, but also on its intellectual and cultural climate. Here a person could think more or less independently, without excessive fear of censure or banishment, although religious sacrilege was met often with stern rebuke. Irascible figures such as Hipponax, whose satiric poems thoroughly scoured the egos of prominent citizens, managed to remain fixtures in Ephesus. Thriving in the community were a variety of religious and intellectual influences from Greece, Egypt, Judea, Persia, Scythia, and the lands beyond the Indus River. The dominant language in the time of Heraclitus was Ionic Greek, the same as on the Attic mainland. Unlike Athens, however, Ephesus would also have had exposure to Lydian, Aeolic, Carian, Mysian, and Doric Greek, as well as Persian, Aramaic, and a variety of Eastern tongues. The net effect of this polyglot of tongues and cultural influences was a high level of tolerance and a high degree of cultural infusion from lands most Greeks would have termed barbaric.

The special significance of the years around 500 B.C., when Heraclitus was in his prime, was that the cultural infusion of new thought characteristic of Ephesus must have reached an apex. Although this thesis is difficult to prove, it is the argument of this book that Heraclitus was exposed to, as well as contributed to, the energy of what the historian Erik Voegelin has named the "Great Leap of Being" and Karl

Jaspers called "The Axial Period." For it was at this point in world history that the culture of myth had sufficiently weakened in its influence to permit new visions of cosmic order and meaning, and what took the place of myth was a wholly new thing in nature. Although Hegel referred in his work to the birth of Christ as the pivotal moment in Western culture, we can say that 500 B.C. was the axis around which world culture really turns.

In 500 B.C. the Buddha, Lao Tse, Confucius, and Zoroaster (Zarathustra) were alive and teaching in the East. There is, of course, some debate about the exact years in question, particularly for the person of Lao Tse, but it is generally accepted that these important religious figures were gradually spreading their investigations, inspirations and instigations into the known world. Voegelin called this period the Great Leap of Being because these teachers effectively changed the consciousness of their cultures and thus of the world. It is highly probable that intimations of this revolution in thought not only reached Ephesus and Heraclitus but were indeed nourished there. The intelligentsia of Ephesian society would have debated the ideas which flowed into the city with the trading parties, perhaps exchanging scrolls as well as stories coming from afar. We know, for example, that the writings of Heraclitus reached Athens in the time of Euripides, where his thought was debated among the elite of the city and later became crucial to the development of Plato's thought. So, too, Eastern thought must have entered Ionian consciousness in the same way.

Of particular importance at the end of the sixth century B.C. was the emergence in India of Advaita Vedanta, the non-dualistic religion based on the Hindu Vedas, which were first written down from oral tradition in the eighth or seventh centuries B.C. Vedanta was a philosophic/religious movement that confronted the heterodox beliefs of the Indus basin and emphasized the individual's autonomous role in transcending the superficial dualism of ordinary existence. Advaita teaches that the human self (*atman* in Sanskrit) is identical to the soul of all things (Brahman). In our own time the foremost philosopher of Vedanta was Sri Aurobindo (Aurobindo Ghose, 1872-1950), whose useful essay on the similarities between Heraclitus and Vedanta was written in 1916-17.[1] It is certainly possible that the main tenets of Vedanta found their way to Ephesus in the sixth century B.C. If not, the similarities between the fragments and Vedanta suggest a strong argument for the emergence of similar thought spread over a wide area of the civilized world.

* * *

Although we must certainly regard biographical legends about Heraclitus with caution, we can accept that he was born into a noble family and at some point abdicated his role in the leadership of the city-state in favor of a life of self-reflection. Whether or not he officially relinquished his patrimony, which might have included rule of Ephesus, to his brother, cannot be known for certain. But something touched him and drew him into a life of introspection and subsequently into teaching, for surely he had followers who promulgated his thought to the Greek world.

That he chose to live as a hermit, away from the life in the city, is virtually certain. Ephesus is surrounded by wooded mountains, home to numerous caves, streams, springs, and supplies of nuts, berries and wildlife. A hermit could have survived quite well in this environment. As well, students or followers would have kept their master in food and clothing. One account suggests, in fact, that Heraclitus lived in a hut equipped with a stove. One day, when students approached the door and looked in, the master was standing

---

1. Sri Aurobindo, *Heraclitus*, Sri Aurobindo Ashram, Pondicherry, India, 1989.

by the stove, and when he saw their hesitation, said, "Do not fear, the gods are here also."

Previous examinations of the thought of Heraclitus confine the contextual circumstances to Attic culture. Given the history of Athens, which in the time of Heraclitus experienced the reforms of Cleisthenes and the intellectual and spiritual advances of Pythagoras, that context seems to this observer to be too narrow. If the thesis of the polyglot culture of Ephesus holds and Heraclitus was indeed exposed to the influences of the East, his thought as found in the extant fragments reflects an authentic fusion of Eastern and Western philosophical and spiritual traditions. The main effect of that fusion would have been a synthesis of concepts of unity, or non-dualism, from the Eastern worlds and multiplicity from the Western, out of which grew a unique transformative vision.

Heraclitus wanted us to know how the One manifested itself in the Many and how the Many held within it the One. It is a question that intrigues modern physics and evolutionary biology today. How did "all this" come from a single point, what we now call a Big Bang? How did the diversity of life arise from a single cell? What are the laws which govern multiplicity as a natural and lawful expression of the fundamental unity? Before Heraclitus could address similar questions, however, he had to grasp the concept of unity, or the One. Such a concept did not arise in traditional Greek religion or mythology. It is not, for example, contained in the *Theogony* of Hesiod, in Homeric epics, or, for that matter, even in the *Golden Verses* of Pythagoras. Nor does it appear in Orphic thought or the Eleusinian Mysteries.

The One Supreme Self, or *paramatman*, is Vedic in origin and is central to Eastern thought. Its pervasive influence became overt for the first time in the eighth century B.C. with the Upanishads. In these great verses, the Supreme Self stands separate and alone in contrast to the world of change or mutability. This Supreme or Absolute Self is beyond time and space and does not act in any traditional sense of action in the realm of causality. As we shall see below, it informed the concept of the Logos in the fragments and also informed the Logos of the Gospel of St. John.

To clarify the point, what follows is an approximate time line showing the infusion of influences in both Western and Eastern traditions. The juxtaposition of influences may serve as a corrective to the habit of separating these traditions in intellectual and religious history.

Historical Parallels	
c. 1300 B.C. Moses	c. 1500–800 Vedas
c. 900 Solomon	*Brahmanas* (prose commentaries) Parsva (Jaina Savior)
800–500 Hebrew Prophets	c. 800–700 Upanishads
c. 800 Homer	Early Indian Hero Epics Kapila (founder of Sankhya)
c. 775 Hesiod	
c. 640–546 Thales	Mahavira (Jaina Savior)
c. 611–547 Anaximander	Gosala (rival of Buddha)
c. 582–500 Pythagoras	563-483 Buddha
c. 500 **Heraclitus**	c. 500–200 Advaita Vedanta
c. 500 B.C. Biblical Genesis written down from oral tradition	c. 500 B.C. −100 A.D. Sutras

The fragments of Heraclitus certainly do not represent a religious movement or, for that matter, a systematic philosophy. Heraclitus does deserve, however, to rank high among the important figures of a crucial era of religious and philosophical development. He is central to the long line of thinkers who trace the thread of Unity through Western culture, including Pythagoras, Empedocles, Plato, Epicurus, Plotinus, St. Augustine, Meister Eckhart, Marcilio Ficino, Jacob Boehme and on to include the Romantic and Transcendental idealists of the modern era. Some might argue that the obscurity of the fragments lends them to almost any tradition, as is evidenced by their inclusion in the works of Aristotle and later thinkers of his rational school. But in fact, Heraclitus truly belongs among those concerned with human transformation. He is less concerned with society and the laws of nature than with inner truth and the discovery of the ways in which human beings can effect a kind of alchemical transformation of their being to bring that being into communion with the Supreme or Absolute Self.

It is within this latter sense that the work of Heraclitus is esoteric. He wrote for a spiritual and philosophic aristocracy and intended his words to be understood only by those who were prepared to take advantage of their transformational intent, although it may be true that those men and women could have arisen from any place or status in the culture. He obviously cherished what he called the *aristoi*, those of his culture who were prepared by background, natural ability, and spiritual inclination to explore and aspire to his expanded vision. His separation from the ordinary world, including the normative Ephesian society and politics, signaled his esoteric intentions and made his own spiritual progress possible.

The meaning of the word esoteric in this context is important to the progress through the argument of this text. Among the possible denotations of the word, including abstruse, arcane, or obscure (a word often associated with Heraclitus), the relevant synonyms are privileged and inner. Many of the fragments suggest strongly that when Heraclitus chose to write down his oracular thoughts, he did so in a manner that precluded their abuse in popular thought or in ordinary opinion. It is in that sense that they were seen as riddles. Socrates himself, when asked if he had read Heraclitus, replied that although what he had understood impressed him, it would take a Delian diver to comprehend the rest. The pearl hunters from the island of Delos were famous for diving great depths and holding their breath for long periods in order to bring valued treasures to the surface. The fragments as treasures are deep, hidden, tightly held, and elusive.

The sense of esoteric as an inner tradition would also have corresponded to the mystery religions in archaic Ionia. But by the time of Heraclitus, the mysteries, with the possible exception of those in Eleusis, had been corrupted as collective experiences. The Orphic traditions would have narrowed by this time to more autonomous spiritual and intellectual explorations. When Heraclitus said, **I searched my nature,** he affirmed the primacy of personal inner reflection, of searching within in order to rid the mind of erroneous sense impressions and empty opinions. Some prefer to translate that fragment as "I searched for myself," which carries a connotation of studying for one's own knowledge and benefit to the exclusion of the broad culture or for one's place in history. Either translation is correct grammatically, but only one can reflect the author's intent. The first seems to be more attuned to the other fragments because it contains a core of intriguing ambiguity centered on self-reflection.

In addition to the term esoteric and the difficulties it might present for us in a post-modern intellectual context, there is also the term transformation. When we speak of transformation in a religious context, the term suggests transfiguration and reformation. In the inner traditions, the term more nearly suggests fundamental change in perception and outlook, combined, perhaps, with a fundamental change in being, which in turn is connected to a more or less permanent alteration in consciousness. For Heraclitus the idea of transformation finds itself represented in many of the fragments. Indeed, as we follow the notion of Heraclitus as an instigator through the fragments, we notice right away that they are composed and phrased in such a way as to instigate a transformation of awareness. Reflected upon in this light, the fragments change the being, unless, of course, one consciously defends against their influence by putting up one's skeptical guard.

The way in which these fragments accomplish this transformation within the willing seeker is akin to alchemy. In the context of 500 B.C., as opposed, for example, to the Medieval period, alchemy meant for Heraclitus an examination of the interaction of the four fundamental elements of nature: fire (always first and foundational), then earth, air, and water. Already, his Ionian precursors, Thales, Anaximander, and Anaximenes had made a series of more secular or naturalistic statements about the four elements, even though they expressed their views in expansive and abstract terms. Their statements nonetheless are also remarkably alchemical, that is, in the strict sense of delving into the secrets of nature for the purpose of understanding the relationship between human and divine nature. In a very real sense, the images that we have of Medieval alchemy reflect accurately the life that Heraclitus no doubt led: secret and lonely searching, inner reflection based on the laws and manifestations of nature, and, most important, the emphasis on fire as a transforming energy.

In the biographical legend referring to his students arriving to see their master at his stove, for example, Heraclitus says to them, "Do not fear, the gods are here also." This otherwise innocuous invitation has come down to us through two millennia. Why? It appears on its surface only to suggest that the followers of Heraclitus were very cautious about disturbing their master while he was either making soup or warming himself. Neither explanation is useful or worthy of recording. If, on the other hand, we suppose that Heraclitus was busy at his stove experimenting with the properties of fire, his students might well have hung back until reassured that this dangerous-looking activity, too, should properly be considered as divine inquiry.

Connecting Heraclitus to alchemy is not a simple or obvious matter. The only real evidence that later alchemists looked back at Heraclitus to support their work emerges in references to the fragments in their own writings. For example, the Arab alchemist Khalid (c. 660-704 A.D.) mentions Heraclitus in several places in his copious notes. Indeed, the biographical details of figures like Khalid who were engaged in highly esoteric experimentation are remarkably similar to those surrounding Heraclitus.

We are also told by the ancient biographers of Heraclitus that he was born into a high social and political position and that at some stage in his life he turned his back on kingship and became a misanthrope. The Hellenic commentators in particular may be forgiven this last excess. In their world, any denial of a hereditary position of power would have been met with incredulity and cynical dismissal. To relinquish one's hereditary place in the hierarchy of community was unthinkable. Nothing was more important than serving in the proper position destined by one's birth. The human being was totally integrated into the *polis* in every way. Indeed, prior to the modern era, no person was fully able to stand existentially outside the community as an individual and still survive. The failure of Socrates to do so was the most famous example. As a result, commentators from the Hellenistic and Roman eras could only assume from some of the fragments critical of leaders in Ephesus that Heraclitus had misanthropic tendencies.

We can say now, more objectively, that at some point in his life Heraclitus must have made a decision to withdraw from active political life and dedicate himself instead to philosophical inquiry. The resulting wisdom of his observations and the importance of their impact on subsequent thought do not suggest a fundamental disgust with society or his fellow human beings. Some of the observations are harsh, to be sure, but then the need for complete separation from the mundane was also imperative. For Heraclitus, human beings were capable of so much more than was evident in their normal behaviors and ordinary levels of understanding. After examining himself, he concluded that both he and others of similar knowledge were capable of attaining to a higher, more unified level of being. The cost of such transformation was withdrawal from the culture. How complete was the withdrawal is probably a matter of taste.

In this sense, Heraclitus is part of the Hermetic and esoteric movements of the pre-Socratic era. As has already been said, the term esoteric in this context refers to the realm of the adept, the relation between a master and his disciples for the purpose of attaining to a higher level of knowledge, understanding and being. It has been more common for the modern observer looking back to pre-Socratic philosophy to limit this level of esoteric participation to Empedocles and Thales in addition to the more obvious figure of Pythagoras, whose school and spiritual practices give evidence of esoteric content. For Heraclitus we have no similar evidence. I would argue, however, that the fragments, in their tone and syntax, strongly suggest an esoteric teaching and that Heraclitus had numerous followers. We do have evidence from commentators such as Clement of Alexandria that there were as many followers of Heraclitus, as there were of Pythagoras. This so-called "following" would have been more than just those who took up the methods of observation of the master. They would have been those who believed in a method of transformation and who used the instigating sayings of their master to inquire into human existence and being.

The purpose of giving serious attention to dubious biographical data is to explore the possible track that the master might have followed in his efforts to achieve a different and more elevated being. Most modern commentators attribute the oddness of the biographical data to jealousy or to misunderstanding, the former being the more probable. If we look, however, at the details of the various accounts of his life, we may find clues to its more esoteric nature. In other words, perhaps Heraclitus followed a regimen of study and daily existence that makes absolute sense in terms of esoteric disciplines as much as it makes no sense at all in more ordinary terms.

The following biographical account is taken from the Loeb Classical Library, *Hippocrates*, Volume iv, which contains the W. H. S. Jones translations of the fragments. The biography is taken from the R. D. Hicks translation of Diogenes Laertius' account of the life of Heraclitus.

Heraclitus, son of Bloson or, according to some, of Heracon, was a native of Ephesus. He flourished in the 69th Olympiad.[2] He was lofty-minded beyond other men, and over-weaning, as is clear from his book in which he says, "Much learning does not teach understanding; else it would have taught Hesiod, Pythagoras, or, again, Xenophanes and Hecataeus." For "this one thing is wisdom, to understand thought[3], as that which guides all the world everywhere."

---

2. 504-500 B.C. This is the primary reference in dating Heraclitus. Nothing is known of his birth or death, except that he may have lived to the age of sixty. If prime is forty, he may have died in 480 BCE, just the beginning of the classical period.

And he used to say that Homer deserved to be chased out of the lists and beaten with rods, and Archilochus[4] likewise.

Again he would say: "There is more need to extinguish insolence than an outbreak of fire," and "The people must fight for the law as for city-walls." He attacks the Ephesians, too, for banishing his friend Hermodorus: he says: "The Ephesians would do well to end their lives, every grown man of them, and leave the city to beardless boys, for that they have driven out Hermodorus, the worthiest man among them, saying, "We will have none who is worthiest among us; or if there be any such let him go elsewhere and consort with others." And when he was requested by them to make laws, he scorned the request because the state was already in the grip of a bad constitution. He would retire to the temple of Artemis and play at knuckle-bones with the boys; and when the Ephesians stood round him and looked on, "Why you rascals," he said, "are you astonished? Is it better to do this than to take part in your civil life?"

Finally, he became a hater of his kind and wandered in the mountains, and there he continued to live, making his diet of grass and herbs. However, as this gave him dropsy, he made his way back to the city and put this riddle to the physicians, whether they were competent to make a drought after heavy rain. They could make nothing of this, whereupon he buried himself in a cowshed, expecting that the noxious damp humor would be drawn out of him by the warmth of the manure. But, as even this was of no avail, he died at the age of sixty.[5]

---

3. "Thought" in this context comes closer to the Enlightenment concept of Reason than "idea" — RGG.

4. An early poet (750 B.C.) known for his invective and parodies. Little remains of his work.

5. Other biographers deny this account of his death, but all seem to agree that he was buried in the agora, or market-place at Ephesus.

Most commentators claim that the above represents the vituperation of jealous contemporaries, who found in the book left by Heraclitus enough obscurity to whet their whimsical fancies. Another interpretation is that the details in the biography are taken loosely from the fragments themselves and were strung together to make up a fanciful litany of events, this to compensate for the paucity of authentic details. The fact remains that once Heraclitus left the political stage, his biography would be slight in any case. Very few of the pre-Socratic thinkers left personal data of any kind. It is a fact of life that we know more about Pericles than we do about Socrates or Plato for these same reasons.[6]

Another possible interpretation of these unseemly details is that they reflect some esoteric theme. Each event serves to tell the story of an adept who turned his back on normal life and took the narrow path to personal enlightenment and transformation. His explorations would look very much like the ranting and raving of a misanthrope, even to the details of retiring to the mountains to eat grass and herbs. As we know from the account in the Book of Daniel of King Nebuchadnezzar eating grass, the image serves a useful purpose in describing a lapse into madness. In his case, although the evidence is strong that no such episode ever took place for him either, it is more likely that what we have are tall tales which naturally evolve when an individual assumes a lifestyle deviant from the norm. Given the extraordinary power of the fragments and the devotion to Heraclitus paid by 2,500 years of intellectual inquiry, we can dismiss with confidence any idea that he lost his mind. What is much more probable from the evidence is that in fact he found it.

---

6. In ancient times, kings and tyrants were the only ones able to afford biographers. It is remarkable that the historian Thucydides included so much of the context of the life of Pericles in his coverage of the Peloponnesean War.

The effort to re-assemble or re-member the fragments of Heraclitus is an attempt, then, to extrapolate from the remains and arrive at what the whole might have said or meant as serious and eminently sensible philosophy. There remains, fortunately, enough of a style and a core of meaning to give a strong sense of what the whole must have sounded like and even meant. It is hoped that by openly speculating about possible meaning, the reader will feel bold enough to strike out independently into wholly new territories.

Influence

The final effort to "re-member" this obscure figure through his fragmentary remains can legitimately be aided by considering his impressive legacy, not merely in the accounts left by commentators, but in the substance and development of the philosophical enterprise after 500 B.C. In modern times, Hegel was not only an admirer, but claimed that Plato was a student of Heraclitus and was much influenced by him. If we accept that assessment, we are able to see how the essential themes of Plato's work reflect back on the master. Not only does *anamnesis* have its roots in the Heraclitean vision of the Logos underlying sensory experience, but so too is the very dialectic itself rooted in the instigations of his oracular voice.

In Plato's famous second letter, he warns his student Dionysius about the dangers of exposing esoteric teachings to those not prepared to hear them. I take this opportunity to quote the relevant passage in full, as it is so strongly reflective of what Heraclitus, too, would have said:

Take precautions, however, lest this teaching ever be disclosed among untrained people, for in my opinion there is in general no doctrine more ridiculous in the eyes of the general public than this, nor on the other hand any more wonderful and inspiring to those naturally gifted. Often repeated and

constantly attended to for many years, it is at last like gold
with great effort freed from an alloy. Let me tell you, however, the surprising thing about it. There are men, and a good
many of them too, who have intelligence and memory and
the ability to judge a doctrine after examining it by every
possible test, who are now old men and have been receiving
instruction not less than thirty years, who have just reached
the point of saying that what formerly they thought most
uncertain, now appears to them quite certain and evident,
while what seemed most certain then, appears now uncertain. Consider these facts and take care lest you sometime
come to repent of having now unwisely published your
views. It is a very great safeguard to learn by heart instead of
writing. It is impossible for what is written not to be disclosed. That is the reason why I have never written anything
about these things, and why there is not and will not be any
written work of Plato's own. What are now called his are the
work of a Socrates embellished and modernized.[7]

When Plato states unequivocally that he "has never written anything about these things," we have the right to wonder what was the daily work of the Academy. His claim that
all he did was to embellish and modernize the teaching of
Socrates suggests that the great dialogues do not, strictly
speaking, constitute a teaching. The true work of the Academy, at least while Plato was its master, was more Heraclitean, that is, it must have been devoted to uncovering the
mysteries of the Logos and developing in students the discipline and mastery of the examined life.

We would not say, however, that the Academy was similar to the Brotherhood of Pythagoras, which was more of a

---

7. *The Collected Dialogues of Plato*, ed. Edith Hamilton and Huntington
Cairns, Bollingen Series LXXI, Princeton University Press, Princeton, 1961,
p. 1567.

communal school or sect following a rigorous life of study and spiritual practice. Nor do we have evidence that Heraclitus founded such a school, although it is, as we have said, highly probable that he had devoted followers and/or students. Nonetheless, the strong possibility that Plato possessed the work of Heraclitus and that he used it as a basis for the hidden or esoteric work of the Academy is highly likely.

We then ask, if Plato is correct in admonishing his friend not to write down the teaching, why did Heraclitus himself, following a similar principle, choose to write a book, to risk exposing his ideas to those unprepared to receive them? One answer is that what Heraclitus deposited in the sanctuary of Artemis was sufficiently cryptic to baffle those who were incapable of grasping its core ideas. If it is the case that we are shielded from what we are not yet ready to see, then the book of Heraclitus was safe in the hands of fools and would serve only to insult those citizens of Ephesus whose ignorance and conceit blinded them from its message.

If Aristotle is correct, Plato gradually turned away from Heraclitus and turned for his exoteric work (written dialogues) to Socrates, whose ethical and moral concerns formed the basis of Plato's metaphysics. Aristotle himself employed Heraclitus to his own ends, focusing his investigative attentions on the observations made by Heraclitus into the laws of nature. For Aristotle, the question of unity, that is, the statement that the universe is One (fundamental to Heraclitean vision), was a matter of discovering what that One was as a thing, or substance. His conclusion was expressed in terms of a substance of fine-grained and subtle quality whose closest element was fire. This analysis by Aristotle was somewhat reductive and removed investigative philosophy far afield from the real concerns of Heraclitus, and it would be nearly five hundred years before philosophy returned to the core of his thinking.

In Plotinus the thought of Heraclitus found a new understanding. In his hierarchy of being and theory of emanations, Plotinus established an intellectual principle having clear correspondences with the Heraclitean Logos. Plotinus established a hierarchy beginning with the One (equivalent to Plato's Good), followed by the Intellectual Principle, the Divine Mind, the Embodied Soul, the World-at-Large (as an entity), Humankind, and so on to the level of inanimate being. The presence of the Intellectual Principle and the Divine Mind (*Nous*) has echoes in several fragments, as we shall see. One in particular, Fragment 34, **To be wise is one thing: to know the thought that directs all things through all things**[8] firmly establishes the primacy of thought or mind as the guiding principle of the universe.

Plotinus logically asks how the One may be known. He answers that the human soul, the conscious link to the One, must approach the Divine Mind through a supernatural insight. In order to accomplish this feat, the individual must follow disciplines, simplifying his or her life, being alone and abiding where the One resides and can be known. For Plotinus the flight of the Alone to the Alone is the climactic moment of existence. This analysis of human existence is closer to the Platonic vision and the esoteric work of the Academy than anything we read in the exoteric work of Plato or Aristotle.

After Plotinus, these themes would not appear in philosophy again until the early Renaissance with the work of Marcilio Ficino, whose grasp of Plato and the Neoplatonists informed the thought of the period. After that, the spread of esoteric doctrines into northern Europe was confined to the

---

8. The Greek word *kybernetes*, from which we derive the word 'cybernetics' means literally "helmsman." It is often translated "steer," but the meaning is closer to 'direct' is the sense of conscious control of cosmic activity.

realms of Christian mysticism and alchemic mysteries. From 1500 until the modern era, Aristotle's exoteric doctrines, amplified by Aquinas, were triumphant, and Heraclitus became an obscure figure with a fragmented persona. His work remained unamplified, with his proper connections to Plato and Plotinus severely curtailed.

The argument of this brief book is that such a destiny is both undeserved and unfortunate, since we, who currently flounder in the post-modern effluent of the past two centuries, are badly in need of new impulses and significant renewal. If Hegel ends the philosophical debate, with Wittgenstein supplying the coup de grace, how are we to proceed? When Heraclitus said **I searched my nature,** he left a clue. When he also said, **Listening to the Logos and not to me, it is wise to agree that all things are One,** he established a principle by which and through which we may be able to find again a place to stand.

Apophasis

In the Greek, *apophasis* means denial or negation and is, therefore, a fitting place to begin to examine the aversive thought of Heraclitus. As used conceptually in philosophy and theology *apophasis* has the connotation of affirmation through negation, as reflected in Negative Theology, a movement that in the Greek tradition usually begins with Plato and reaches its apex with Plotinus and Proclus. For the Greeks, apophatic theology involved disposing of the myths of the Olympian gods while affirming a revised vision of the Unknown God, the unreachable, unmanifest but immanent deity.

Scholars of Negative Theology, including in particular A. H. Armstrong, reach back from Plato to Parmenides among the pre-Socratics for the well-springs of Negative Theology. In general Heraclitus is not mentioned, mostly, it would seem, because the fragments are not theologically compatible with Christian assumptions, or not sufficiently so. And yet, more than any other pre-Socratic thinker, Heraclitus embodies the apophatic method. He "unsaid" the myths of the Archaic tradition on his way to transforming the ideas of divinity through the divine Logos. It was a transformation affirmed by Plotinus eight hundred years later.

Apophatic reasoning and imagery work together to penetrate the layers of encrusted myth-making which conceal the bright light of an original truth. Eventually the covering obscures the truth of reality altogether to create its own illusory design. The myths of Hesiod and Homer as applied to religious thought and belief were such illusory coverings. Straightforward myth-making always embellishes, whereas apophatic imagery strips away. The interpreters of embellishing myth create attractive landscapes of metaphor and explanation, whereas the apophatic philosopher works in more blunt, abstract imagery. As a result it is seldom a comfort to the believer to be exposed to Negative Theology, at least not in the sense of comfort as solace. The intent is often to shock or to awaken a new sensibility. Such was the work and the suffering of Meister Eckhart, for example, which dispelled a thousand years of encrusting myth that obscured the original light of Christianity. Similarly, the reputation of Heraclitus as a misanthrope was certainly due in part to his apophasis.

The Greek word for truth, *aletheia,* consists of the prefix *a,* not, and *lethe,* forgetfulness or forgetting. Thus even truth-telling has an aversive cast, being a process of not-forgetting, as opposed to the more affirmative sense in the word knowing. When Heraclitus tells us in Fragment 15 that Nature prefers to hide he expresses that sense of uncovering or un-forgetting, which characterizes our search for the truth of reality.

Heraclitus and the other pre-Socratics unraveled centuries of Greek myth-making in blunt, often shocking directness. As we shall see in his vision of the Logos, Heraclitus challenges us to understand through negation, telling us what the Logos is not and yet what still may be affirmed from the myth. In Fragments 51 and 52, for example, he engages the Delphic tradition in order to unsay much of its mythical covering. **The raving Sibyl, through the god, utters somber, unembellished, unperfumed sayings, reaching over a thousand years with her voice.** (Fragment 52)

"Raving" illustrates the nature of divine utterance in its prototypical form. The transcription into ordinary sentences is necessarily a distortion. In other words, human sentence-making automatically obscures the light. The pattern of communication at Delphi called for the Sibyl to utter whatever impulses she received as inspiration. Her utterances or "ravings" were then civilized into hexameters by the priests for delivery to the supplicant. That essential light was lost in translation is obvious. Indeed, as the Delphic mysteries became corrupted during and following the classical period, a supplicant could receive favorable translation for a price. Obscurity became deception or obfuscation.

Even for honest framers, however, the utterances of the Sibyl adorned the unembellished utterance like an elaborate covering. What then were these utterings in the first place? What truth did they contain? In the great tradition of "Know Thyself," the reminder which greeted supplicants in the sanctuary at Delphi, the utterances of the god were signs to be interpreted by human awareness and understanding.

Fragment 51 clarifies the intent. **The divine one whose oracle is in Delphi speaks neither directly or obscurely, but rather gives a sign**. This negation, while dismissing other options, leaves the sign, an indication of a direction of meaning. The message was not "maybe yes, maybe no," but was more like the readings of the *I Ching*, the Chinese Book of Changes, in which a question posed by the supplicant is answered by an indication, which, if we are wise, may be translated into an appropriate direction. Signs show the way but do not describe the destination.

These two fragments illustrate much of the style and import of the rest of the Heraclitean fragments. They are signs. They speak neither directly or obscurely, although many would argue the latter point. Known by many commentators as "The Obscure," Heraclitus confounds most readers because they come to him with deep-seated opinions and beliefs and are shocked and offended by the fragments. What they take away from the fragments is that sense of offense. But if we understand his intent and remain open to it, we can come closer to understanding the signs. Heraclitus' "ravings" are somber, unembellished, and unperfumed, a perfect illustration of sibylline utterance.

If the fragments of Heraclitus resemble the oracular methods of the Sibyl, the question arises as to the source of his utterances. Fragment 53 unsays much of the sources of our so-called knowledge. In **I searched my nature,** Heraclitus tells us about his own inquiries. We tend to search for answers to life's problems everywhere but within, everywhere but in the recesses of our nature where true patterns and laws are to be found. **I searched my nature** is a sign telling where to search for reality. Within our own Delphic nature lies hidden all the essential laws of the cosmos and of manifest nature. The signs of the Logos for which we search are contained within and yet they are also everywhere.

The sayings of the god reverberate within and we hear, or not, as the case may be. In this way **I searched my nature** negates the traditional external search for knowledge but does not deny the rigors of the scientific or dialectical method. Search we must, but we must be aware of our sources and of the nature of the signs we uncover. If we begin with outmoded or encrusted signs, we have little chance of success.

Hesiod gave the Greeks the traditional myth of creation and the gods. His story of the *Theogony* is long and violent. Out of Chaos came the male and female gods, manifestations of consciousness in the cosmos, procreating through the power of Eros, which is the force through which the green fuse drives the flower, as Dylan Thomas had it, and is also the manner in which all spiritual knowledge is transmitted. Hesiod's is the account of the turbulence of the creative forces unleashed out of the primal mystery, some of which are transmitted to humanity. There are the conflicts of power, the temptations of selfish desires, and the depravity of destructive instincts. Also in the birth of the minor gods, such as Blame and Woe, the powers are released, such as when Blame grows untended by Reason into the Night, enlarged by Dreams into injustice and ruthless vengeance.

In a masterful negation of Hesiod, Heraclitus unsays the myth. Fragment 24 recreates the foundations of cosmology.

This cosmos (the unity of all that is) **was not made by immortal or mortal beings, but always was, is and will be an eternal fire, arising and subsiding in measure**. Commencing with a firm "was not," the fragment is a myth-penetrating assertion of the eternal nature of the cosmos. No beginning, no end. Mystery. Denied here is the god-creator of Genesis (already a flourishing text in the time of Heraclitus) and Hesiod's *Theogony*. And yet, and here is the uncovering to the core, the Logos, as fire, was, is and will be present as the cosmos arises and subsides in measure (*metron*).

The metaphysical problem is clear enough. Five hundred years later, the Apostle John would assert that "In the beginning was the Word" (*Logos*). "In the beginning" does imply a point in time. The Word, John says, was with God "in the beginning," thus affirming God's creation of the cosmos out of chaos. Chaos, of course, may imply random matter present always, and may coincide with the Heraclitian view of "arising and subsiding in measure," but still, Heraclitus asserts that no god, at least, no Olympian god, was involved. In Hindu theogony, universes arise and go out each time Brahma opens his third eye, implying that the god is eternally present and creative. As we shall see later, Heraclitus implies that the Logos as fire was the eternal, infinite source. "Fire" can be expressive of energy present as potential as well as effect. Thus, the argument can be made that all these expressions describe the formation and creative evolution of the cosmos.

Heraclitus asserts negatively that the cosmos — the All, the One, the Logos — ever was, is, and will be, and although this eternal fire will arise and subside in cycles, the cycle will always repeat itself. The very latest cosmology seems to agree that even the so-called Big Bang may not have been the beginning of anything except the formation of our particular universe, which one day may "subside" or collapse in on itself only to "arise" again, or it may be one of many such universes engaged in the same rhythm.[9] Whether or not this particular universe will continue to expand "forever" is by no means a theory commonly held. The point, however, is not to test Heraclitus against present knowledge or theory but rather to reflect how the fragment negates tradition while affirming his vision of the Logos, which we will examine in the next chapter.

Fragment 30 explores this cosmological problem further. **What we call 'hot' seems to be immortal and to apprehend all things: to see and hear and know all things, both present and future. This otherness, then, the diversity of the all, when things become clouded, went out to the furthermost revolution, and seems to me to have been what was called ether by the men of old.** This "hot" becomes the metaphor for Fire, which in turn will find for Heraclitus its identification as the Logos. A century later, Anaxagoras will subsume the Logos into his vision of the Nous, or Mind, saying about it that it is infinite, unmade, self-ruled, and alone by itself. For him, Mind was everywhere, infusing the cosmos with creative intelligence and consciousness. His was a crucial step which could not have been taken without Heraclitus.

Fragment 35 completes this process of unsaying the myths of Hesiod. **The One, the only wisdom, does and yet does not consent to be called Zeus.** This simultaneous naming and unnaming of the god corresponds to all later negative theology, right up to and including Maimonides and Eckhart in the Jewish and Christian mystical traditions. When Eckhart famously said, "I pray to God that I may be free of God," he confronts that paradox. The "only wisdom" is an approximation of the unknown and unknowable

---

9. Superstring theory posits the existence of multiple universes within multiple dimensions — at least ten. Even black holes present the possibility of other universes of anti-matter and worm-hole travel to and from multiple dimensions.

god, at once transcendent and immanent. In effect, God *says,* "give me a name if you wish but not attributes. I am that I am."

As the next chapter will name, The One becomes the Logos for Heraclitus, or more precisely, the One becomes the wisdom partially known through the Logos, which is one with it. The fiery Logos in effect names what cannot be named and knows what cannot be known. This double knowing and unknowing finds its expression for Heraclitus in the phrase "does and does not consent." It is through the *apophatic* paradox that we come to know the unknowable. Through negation we come to know something positively.

Why is this? Why should it be so that through aversive thinking we can arrive at affirmation? Partly, it is because genius rebels from the received tradition, not because it is inherently wrong by being the tradition, but because we learn, as Ralph Waldo Emerson understood so well, not from instruction but from provocation. True teaching provokes in the student an intuition of the truth, but because it is provocation, there follows an aversive reaction in the one so provoked.

All those phrases among the fragments which express the paradox of knowing through unknowing come together now: "Listen to the Logos and not to me," "The path up and the path down are the same," whole but not whole," "brought together and taken apart," "in tune and out of tune," "out of all things a unity . . . out of unity all things," "how being in conflict it agrees," "and last, Fragment 17: **If we do not expect the unexpected we will not discover it, since it is not to be searched out and is difficult to apprehend.**

What must our mental state be in order to expect the unexpected? How can we search without searching? The "it" in this fragment must be the Logos, and if we are to apprehend it, we must not be too expectant, searching methodically. And yet, we must be prepared (in some state of unconscious alertness) to receive the unexpected gifts of the Logos, which flow to us everywhere and yet nowhere.

Apophasis, then, provides us with an important mental stance in preparation for approaching all of the fragments. Our thinking must be aversive. It is what Heidegger meant in *What is Called Thinking* when he referred to the thinking process as "from the start tuned in a negative key."[10] Genius revises, smashes the old jars, chips away the accumulated crust obscuring the core truths of existence.

The real importance of Heraclitus lies not so much in his insights into the nature of reality, as startling and profound as those are, but in his method of exploration. If we are able to emulate in some small way his aversive thinking, his willingness to ridicule while still affirming, and his courage in calling a fool a fool, we have a chance to join his company, even for a short time. It is a company made up of those who are awake, expectant, prepared and most of all dedicated to the road to truth, wherever it might lead.

Fragment 45 provides a last warning about our myth-making tendencies. **Human beings are carried away by every new theory.** The attention which should be focused on knowing ourselves is whipped away by the attractions of new ideas and easy solutions to intractable problems. As doctors know, patients want the newest drug because it is new, and when it becomes an old drug, it no longer works.

---

10. Martin Heidegger, *What is Called Thinking?*, Harper Row, New York, 1968, p. 29.

LOGOS

Although little is certain about the biography of Heraclitus or about the full text of the material which served as the source of his fragments, we do have some certainty about a beginning. The long fragment usually numbered 1 in most translations is quoted by three commentators, including Aristotle and Hippocrates. Our version comes from Sextus Empiricus, the Graeco-Roman philosopher who lived in Alexandria and Rome between 200 and 300 A.D. and wrote a book entitled *Against the Mathematicians*. After quoting Fragment 1 Sextus indicates that "later on," (hence placed as Fragment 2) Heraclitus says, **Therefore it is necessary to obey the universal; but although the Logos is universal, most people live as though they had a private understanding.** It is this reference to "later on" that has convinced scholars that Heraclitus wrote a book, or at least a collection of philosophical statements meant to form a coherent thesis, even a summation of a life's work. It is also quite possible that a student or follower of Heraclitus set down all he could remember of the master's sayings after his death, as was the case with Buddhist texts. It is worth remembering that in the Archaic Period, human memory was a well-developed faculty, and it would not have been difficult to record a collection of the master's more trenchant statements.

Although Fragment 1 may not be the actual opening lines of such a book or collection, it will serve us as a ground of inquiry for two reasons. First, it refers to the Logos in a way that is more fully developed than other references, and second, it serves as the best example of Heraclitus the provocative teacher, illustrating that he probably spent a good deal of time working with students who sought his wisdom and understanding. Fragment 1 shows how difficult the process of philosophical investigation is and to what extent human beings succumb to sleep in this challenging process. He begins:

> The Logos, (which is) as I describe, proves incomprehensible, both before it is heard and even after it is heard. For although all things happen according to the Logos, many act as if they have no experience of it, even when they do experience such words and action as I explain, as when I separate out each thing according to its nature and state how it is; but as to the rest, they fail to notice what they do after they wake up, just as they forget what they do when they sleep.

Whatever the nature of the Logos, it is not self-evident as a part of human experience. We do not grasp it through normal intellectual inquiry, so hidden is it. And then once we have been introduced to it or have had it described to us by example, we still do not understand it, even though all things happen according to its laws or its nature. Last, so dense are we that even when physically awake we do not have the ability to grasp the workings or nature of the Logos. What, then, are we to do?

The hint Heraclitus gives us is that the Logos is apprehended only in a specially wakened state best arrived at through intuitive reflection and self-searching as he reminds us in the enigmatic Fragment 53, **I searched my nature.** Our task is to awaken first to the practice of self-reflection and then to wait upon the Logos. A teacher is always useful as an instigator or one who prods, but the work remains ours. In other words, we search on our own and we search on behalf of ourselves.

Whatever its reality, the Logos is central to the philosophy of Heraclitus. It is the fire around which we gather for warmth and light. Either directly or indirectly, more than twenty fragments refer to it, and an understanding of its nature and qualities is crucial to following his line of inquiry. All of his reflections on human nature, the laws of nature and divinity take their light from the Logos.

We might begin first with some scholarly background. In his thorough *Heraklitus, The Cosmic Fragments* (Cambridge, 1962), G. S. Kirk helps us develop a range of interpretations as follows: Logos comes from the Greek root *leg*, which has the sense of "meaning." On one level, then, Logos is simply the meaning of what Heraclitus has to say. If we are content to limit our investigation, we can say that the Logos is merely the *idea* behind Heraclitus' view of the cosmos. But Heraclitus himself warns against this limitation in Fragment 2. Those who do not grasp the Logos must necessarily operate from their own private ideas. A "private understanding" is recognizable as private because it does not hold up to scrutiny by others, particularly over time. A theory proposed by genius becomes the truth when observation over time substantiates it. Einstein's general theory of relativity is an example.

Considering the Logos more deeply, Holscher and Snall proposed that Logos had the sense of "oracular response," placing it within the Delphic tradition. Since we see in other fragments that Heraclitus respects the oracular tradition, we need to give ample room to this sense as well. In his analysis, Gignon went further to suggest that Logos meant "the truth in things as revealed in [Heraclitus'] book". The idea of the truth in or within things is consistent with its hidden nature.

Further, qualities of the Logos include that it is common, as in universal; it is a unity; it is an account, the Word, and in Kathleen Freeman's words, "the measure of all things." Other possibilities include "laws of force," and "laws of flux." Diels translates it simply as "the teaching we have before us." [11]

The sense of Logos as "measure" from Freeman is one of the more interesting emanations. The Greek concept of measure (*metron*) is that quality or virtue that maintains order, that balances all things in proper proportion. Seen correctly as a law, such measure suggests a universal principle holding the universe together. As a natural philosopher Heraclitus clearly intuited a unifying principle responsible for the existence and character of the cosmos. Measure maintains the dynamic balance of forces keeping the earth in its constant orbit. If the forces change just slightly and our planet achieves the escape velocity of seven miles per second/per second, we fly off into the cold blackness of space. If we slow too much, we fall into the sun. The harmonizing "measure" gives us our deceptive sense of stillness in motion.

It is part of the traditional vision of Logos as divine creator and sustaining presence that informs Christian usage of the term. Most are familiar with the use of *Logos* in the New Testament Gospel of John. The following is from the Jerusalem Bible.

> In the beginning was the [*Logos*] Word;
> the Word was with God
> and the Word was God.
> He was with God in the beginning.
> Through him all things came to be,
> not one thing had its being but through him.

Logos here is identified with the Christ, as John, writing in Greek for the Greek-speaking world, equates the Logos with Christ as the Word that creates and sustains the universe. This connection supports the view that the Greek

---

11. G.S. Kirk, *Heraklitus, The Cosmic Fragments*, Cambridge University Press, Cambridge, 1962, p. 37-56.

intellectual living in the first century A.D. would have made the connection between the Logos and Christ as the Word of God that sustains the cosmos. In the pagan traditions of the Greek world, Apollo had the same function in relation to Zeus the Father, a relationship going back into the Neolithic past. It is apparent, then, that this Logos is not the invention of Heraclitus, but that it has a long history and was made available to human awareness as a series of images of transcendence.

The next sequence of fragments sets forth the relationship between Logos and this form of human perception. We saw in Fragment 2 that the Logos is common or universal in nature, but that most people (*hoi polloi*) behave as though they had a wisdom of their own. Only the few (*aristoi*) are capable of perceiving its nature and existence. This fragment makes it clear that the truth is never relative, that is, never a private opinion. The Logos is present, is eternal, and resides at the center of all things. To attain wisdom, it is necessary to obey what is universal and not what is private. That Heraclitus and the other "few" have knowledge of what is universal and that the most people do not, raises the uncomfortable specter of elitism.

The intellectual problems created by the idea of a few persons having special knowledge while the majority plod on in ignorance has always been with us. It is not exclusively a postmodern, egalitarian issue tied to political correctness. When individuals like Heraclitus first began to speculate on the problems of nature, existence and the cosmos, there were those who condemned them all as arrogant. Even the term philosopher was invented as a substitute for the earlier term *aletheia* or truth-teller, which was the first name for those who engaged in such speculation.[12] A lover of wisdom could be seen as one who did not necessarily possess any greater

---

12. Ortega y Gasset, *The Origin of Philosophy*, W.W. Norton, New York, 1955.

knowledge than the ordinary individual. Even Socrates insisted that he knew nothing, and still he was hounded to his death by those who envied and feared him.

Part of the biographical tradition surrounding Heraclitus suggests that he was also hounded, if not to death, then certainly away from the centers of power and society in Ephesus. He preferred playing dice with the local children on the temple steps to helping his city revise its laws. He chided the city fathers for banishing a leading citizen because the man, a certain Hermodorus, was the best, he said, and that the city would not have one amongst them who was better than anyone else.[13]

What is it about those who know or who possess knowledge we do not? Surely it is about power, the power of knowledge to avoid suffering, to control events, to attain riches. In the case of philosophical knowledge, the problem may not be related particularly to worldly power, although the Sophists of Classical Athens in 400 B.C. may have used knowledge to gain wealth and power to be sure. No, the issue is how we feel about those who claim to possess knowledge which cannot be proven true by traditional (read scientific) means of evaluation.

In the aphorisms of Heraclitus about the Logos, we have such a case. Even though the evidence of the natural universe seems to demonstrate the existence of lawfulness, with the additional possibility that such lawfulness may well be conscious, no demonstrable source of knowledge appears to prove it. As a result, we are both drawn to and repelled by those who express certainty about so-called transcendental facts. Fully aware of these ambiguous feelings, Heraclitus makes a series of penetrating statements designed to pierce the armor of doubt on the one hand and to shatter illusory opinions on the other. And unlike the later philosophers of logic (such as Hegel) who built arguments so monumental

---

13. See Loeb fragment CXIV, 505.

that we finally succumb to their very size and seeming invulnerability, Heraclitus succeeded in his enterprise by denying logic, by surprising us with astonishing paradoxes, and by avoiding the monumental.

All Things Are One

Fragment 3 establishes the center of the Heraclitean circle of knowledge and insight. **Listening to the Logos and not to me, it is wise to agree that all things are One.**

The important distinction is being drawn here between the teacher's arguments and statements (*doxa*) and the truth of the Logos. Whenever we speak, debate, or engage in conscious reflection, we are taking part in the multiplicity of existence, human and otherwise. In saying 'listening to the Logos and not to me' Heraclitus separates his listeners from their momentary attachment to his own words and, in effect, casts them adrift philosophically. We ask him, "How can we not listen to you? How can we listen to the Logos when we cannot hear it?" One answer to these questions is presented in the second half of the fragment.

If Heraclitus had said only, "It is wise to agree that all things are One" and let it go at that, we would be dealing with a more traditional philosophical statement. Here is an informed opinion (*doxa*), which we can file with other such opinions for later reference. However, Heraclitus calls upon the Logos as his authority, saying, in effect, "Listen to the essence of what I have to say to you." This oracular style tends to remove all the fragments from the realm of argument, and we are asked to accept them as revelation or reject all of them as insupportable opinion.

Similarly, if the fragment had read merely, "All things are One," our attention would be forcefully drawn to the speaker as the authority for the truth of the statement. In the New Testament statement from Jesus, "I am the Way and the

Truth and the Life," for example, no doubt arises about where the authority rests in the statement and no doubt as to whom to follow. Heraclitus, however, says "Do not listen to me." In doing so, the burden of knowing the truth is placed on the listener, not on the speaker. It is we ourselves who are responsible for knowing the truth and for seeking out the depths of experience for hints of the Logos in things, among the Many. Heraclitus himself is not our savior nor our source. Indeed, in matters of knowing the truth, nothing and no one may stand between it and us. No mediator, no incarnation, and no go-between.

Heraclitus insisted that everything (*ta panta*) that exists also partakes of the One, not merely as having come from or emerged from the essential Unity at some moment in time, some beginning, but that everything continues to partake of the One in its present, fluctuating becoming. Being in Becoming, Becoming in Being. This formulation is not only possible, it is absolutely necessary. The form of each thing manifests the one form. As Goethe understood, the tree manifests the inherent form of the single leaf. The perfect leaf yields in space the imperfect tree, which must of necessity adapt to the flux of conditions to its particular circumstances. And yet, no matter its situation and appearance, it still manifests the perfection of its leaf. It manifests what Plato would notate as treeness. The leaf is the Logos of the tree.

Fragment 10 takes the next step in Becoming. Unity or Being is seen in its true complexity and not as a pantheistic whole. We are introduced to the flux of all experience, the constancy of change. **Everything taken together is whole but also not whole, what is being brought together and taken apart, what is in tune and out of tune; out of diversity there comes unity, and out of unity diversity.** Here is the tree again, emerging from the leaf and yet becoming a manifest tree in time and space.

Some may see such a statement as obfuscation, throwing dust into our eyes just as we think we are beginning to see. Again, however, we are being drawn into the flux or chaos of experience while being held steady by the essential unity behind everything. See how the fragment begins. Everything taken together is whole and yet not, because, we learn later, this "everything" is in constant flux, holding and yet not holding, being and becoming, in tune and out of tune.

Heraclitus refines this tension by using the image of the drawn bow or the lyre. In Fragment 16 he continues to speak of those who cannot comprehend the Logos even after it has been introduced. **They do not apprehend how being in conflict it still agrees with itself; there is an opposing coherence, as in the tensions of the bow and lyre.**

The bow and the lyre are perfectly tuned to function in tension, what Heraclitus describes as an opposing (literally a back-stretching) connection. The harmony of function and sound resulting from the tension describes a quality of the Logos crucial to its nature and energy. Just as the earth hurtles through space away from the sun, so it is drawn back into the sun and as a result maintains its harmonious motion, held in orbit by that tension. The warfare between flying away and falling inward results in an eternal (relatively speaking) movement.

The operative Greek word here is *palintropos,* which appears in Fragment 16. I have translated it as "opposing coherence." Others use phrases such as "back-turning connection" or "opposing tensions." In any case, the phenomenon being described, as Heraclitus points out, is the action that takes place when a bow is drawn or that force that maintains tension on the strings of the lyre. Pulling it holds. Drawing tight, it releases. In the lyre, the musical harmony of the strings is created and maintained by this opposing tension. Heraclitus saw that nature too maintains its harmonic coherence in the tension of opposites. This state is the central characteristic of the Logos in its operations.

In Fragments 18 and 19 Heraclitus expands on this principle of tension using the image of strife or war, not as an instrument of foreign policy, but as a fact of existence. He derides those who naively wish for peace in the world in the sense of a release of tensions as not understanding the necessity of conflict in the creation. Fragment 18 reads, **It is necessary to know that conflict is universal and that strife is right, and that all things happen through strife and necessity.** The universality of conflict in all that exists and the fundamental rightness of strife are central to human life as well as to cosmic motion and the workings of nature. A human life comes into being through the lawful strife between a defensive egg and an aggressive sperm. Obviously neither claims victory in the fact of fertilization, as the warfare of embryo growth proceeds immediately and is a unity. The egg is defensive in order to maintain its integrity and to preserve its coherent structure and data. The sperm is aggressive in order to form a union, not to destroy the egg.

In Fragment 19 Heraclitus employs personification in order to establish the natural hierarchy displayed in this tension. **Strife is the father of All That Is and king of All That Is, and some participants he shows as immortal, others as mortal; some he makes slaves, others free.** Instead of seeing gods, heroes, warriors, and slaves in historical circumstances, as is the normative reading, we are shown instead a series of roles played out in the drama, very much as the Hindu text of the Mahabharata displays the drama of warfare when Krishna explains to Arjuna what his duties are in the warfare of life.

> These bodies inhabited by the eternal,
> The indestructible, the immeasurable embodied one,
> Are said to come to an end.

Therefore fight Descendant of Bharata (Arjuna).
He who imagines this (the embodied one) the slayer
And he who imagines this (the embodied one) the slain,
Neither of them understands;
This (the embodied one) does not slay, nor is slain.[14]

We are always reminded, however, that with Heraclitus the real issue lies deeper than mythical, historical action or the strife of nature. The Logos is always the focus of attention and is the ultimate goal (the *telos*) of human understanding. So that we are not deluded into thinking that the surfaces of things, that is, the evidence of our senses alone, will reveal the Logos, we have two fragments to guide our seeing. Fragment 14 says, **A hidden connection is stronger than an apparent one,** and Fragment 15, similarly, **Nature prefers to hide.** In this case we translate *physis* as Nature, whereas Kirk and Raven prefer "the real constitution of things" to suggest that nature as we ordinarily see it is not the meaning of *physis* in the Greek. Obviously, if we "see" nature, how can it be hiding? We resolve this conflict by rendering *physis* as Nature, with a capitalized 'N.'

Diels translates this fragment into German as follows: "Die Natur (das Wesen) liebt es sich zu verbergen," which might well come into English as "The nature of being loves to hide." Diels moves away from nature as manifest world and directs the attention to Nature as essence, to include human nature as well (contained in "being").

The Greek word *physis* always has this sense, particularly after Heraclitus in the literature of the classical fifth century, where the term was often set in opposition to *nomos*, meaning social law and custom. When Heraclitus wishes to speak of human nature alone he uses the word

---

14. *The Bhagavad Gita*, trans. Winthrop Sargeant, Doubleday & Co., New York, 1978, p. 115-117.

ethos, as he does in Fragment 12: **Human nature does not have true judgment, but divine nature does.** Here, human nature (*ethos*) refers more to constitution or disposition, not the *physis* of essence, which is related to, if not fully identified with, the Logos.

Also implied in Fragment 15 is the *intention* to hide. In giving *physis* this conscious desire, Heraclitus does more than merely suggest that the essence of things lies hidden within or beneath the surface. There is an active desire to be hidden, as if it is part of the nature of being not to disclose itself. Jones suggests that *physis* is 'the truth about the universe,'[15] which connects essence with truth and raises the question, Why isn't the truth self-evident? Why does it prefer to hide?

Another question comes first, however. Why is it not sufficient to accept the diversity of ordinary experience as the true nature of existence? To accept such a premise is to accept the universe as fundamentally chaotic and all experience as random or accidental. Human beings, in this scheme, have to be merely accidents of evolution and have no purpose other than what they create as purpose. In nature's terms, then, we are simply sperm and egg carriers; this theory states that the chicken is merely nature's invention to produce another egg, which solves at least one classic conundrum.

Such a view is, of course, prevalent today. It had its adherents in the time of Heraclitus as well. It is the view that gave birth to tragedy and heroic raging against the absent gods. Oedipus looks within, sees chaos and abomination, and blinds himself in existential protest. It is, however, characteristic of the human condition to protest also against the

---

15. W. H. S. Jones, *Hippocrates*, vol. IV. Harvard University Press, Cambridge, 1931, p. 473.

view that chaos rules and that cosmos is an illusion. As Hamlet protested,

> What is a man,
> If his chief good and market of his time
> Be but to sleep and feed? A beast, no more!
> Sure he that made us with such large discourse,
> Looking before and after, gave us not
> That capability and godlike reason
> To fust in us unus'd. (IV. iv, 33-40)

It may be argued, of course, that our "large discourse" is an evolutionary development gained over the millennia for the purpose of survival and that Hamlet might well have applied that fact to his own situation to seize the throne and have done with it, whereas thinking too precisely on the event sealed his fate. No longer having the privilege to contemplate being, he must take part in the world of action and will its eventual outcome. Heraclitus, too, faced a similar moment of decision and made the conscious choice to withdraw from center stage in order to find the truth. He became an *aletheia*, a truth-teller. For Heraclitus and Hamlet, withdrawal from the stage is the first step in discovering the nature of being.

We return, however, from this diversion to the initial question about motive: why does Nature prefer to hide? As human beings discovered hidden in the atom, great power resides within the nature of things. It is the power of creation itself and lies hidden much as, in a more mundane example, certain computer instructions are hidden by their creators to prevent destruction of key files and procedures. Playing with the power of the universe must not lie within the range of normal human disposition. As Lord Acton understood, power corrupts, and absolute power corrupts absolutely. If it is true, as some physicists have speculated, that the potential force within a square centimeter of space could destroy the

Earth, we are fortunate if activating this potential remains out of our grasp.

Knowledge of the existence of the Logos, however, is another story. Our awareness of the existence of this power, particularly as a conscious power, arrived at with the proper wisdom, is no danger to ourselves and in fact enhances our participation in 'the nature of things.' The story of revelation has always had this motive. God proclaims, "I am," yet remains hidden from us.

Eternal Fire

In the historical record, which has the habit of battering serious thinkers into banality, Heraclitus is said to employ the image of fire as the common element of the cosmos. The fire fragments do indeed suggest such a common connection, but they do so much more and carry us into an area of real complexity. Fragment 24 introduces the theme:

> **This cosmos [the unity of all that is] was not made by immortal or mortal beings, but always was, is and will be an eternal fire, arising and subsiding in measure.**

Here, Heraclitus asserts the eternal cycles of appearance and disappearance of the presently existing cosmos, brought into existence through eternal fire and extinguished in turns. Since the nature of the cosmos is flux, both in essence and general action, change is the norm in its workings and in its very existence. One present theory of the universe suggests that it came into existence in a Big Bang and will go out of existence in the Big Crunch.[16] It is a long-term breathing.

---

16. Astronomers lately (1998) have concluded that the universe as we know it will keep on expanding 'forever' and will simply "go out," that is, stars will simply extinguish, leaving a cold dark expanse. The debate about the fate of the universe still rages, however, with no proof of its ultimate end.

The use of "measure" introduces the role of the Logos in this flux or breathing. *Metra* is that power maintaining order in change. In Fragment 25 we are shown an example of how this measure operates in nature.

Fire's alternations: first as sea, and of sea half earth and half lightning dispersed as sea, and measured in the same proportion as existed before it became earth. We have here a fragment of a fragment, and although it may not be complete, a geologist might be able to find his way through it well enough. This too, too solid flesh does indeed resolve itself into a dew, just as the molten earth becomes steam, condenses as water and returns once again vaporized to earth in constant cycles of matter. Heraclitus, again, insists on the presence of measure in process, locating the Logos as source and director. Fragment 26 again makes the same point: **All things equally exchange for fire as does fire for all things, as goods are exchanged for gold and gold for goods.**

For Heraclitus the universe came into existence lawfully, in a harmony which necessitated a hand on the wheel. He expresses this control through the use of the word *kybernetes* in its sense of "guide" or "direct" in several fragments. In Fragment 27: **The lightning directs everything** and Fragment 34: **To be wise is one thing: to know the thought that directs all things through all things.** The image of lightning (*keraunos*), supreme in nature as a symbol of fire, retains the natural image of fire and also evokes the image of Zeus as the supreme deity in the Greek pantheon. Zeus is the fire in the mind, pure consciousness.

Zeus was known as Bright Consciousness and the controlling power among the immortals. His chief symbol was the thunderbolt with which he maintained power in the cosmos. The thunderbolt was, on one level, a symbol of overwhelming energy and heaven-sent warning. That human beings were sometimes killed by flashes of lightning from out of the blue, as it were, added power to the symbolism. Since it is clear that Heraclitus tended to use a philosophical language for the most part devoid of mythical imagery, we can conclude that these rare examples were intended as metaphoric clarifications of his more oracular pronouncements. Those Greeks in the Orphic tradition who understood the relationship of the myth-symbol Zeus to human consciousness would have been able to draw the conclusion that human beings participated in this "steering" in the same measure as they took part in consciousness. The trick was to embody the universal element of fire in the thought and not fall into a private understanding.

"**Lightning directs everything,**" then, is a symbolic statement arising from the vestiges of archaic myth and is overlaid with metaphysical meaning. Had Heraclitus had the language to say, "Consciousness directs the cosmos," he would have expressed the same principle in metaphysical terms (as in Fragment 34), but neither of the words "consciousness" or "cosmos" had the same historical depth or connotative strength in his time. Even the phrase *ta panta*, "all things," for the Greek carried the import of everything we see and know, whereas "cosmos," or world-order, implied a narrower sense of the laws behind all those things.

Fragment 34, **To be wise is one thing: to know the thought that directs all things through all things** anticipates brilliantly the later Greek emphasis upon *Nous* or Mind in the philosophy of Anaxagoras, who was born when Heraclitus was in his prime (c. 500 B.C.). The most famous of the aphorisms of Anaxagoras is "Mind is infinite and self-sustaining, is unmixed, alone, and by itself." Later in this famous passage, he says, "Mind drives the whole revolution, so that it revolved initially, first in a small area and now more widely, and eventually more widely still." This highly prophetic understanding of the expanding universe and the nature of diversity emerged first in a reading of Heraclitus, who introduced to the West the notion of Mind as the driving, controlling force of the cosmos.

Another use seen earlier of the myth-symbol Zeus is found in Fragment 35: **The One, the only wisdom, does and yet does not consent to be called Zeus.** The phrase "the only wisdom" translates the Greek phrase *hen to sophon*, also "the one wise." A careful distinction is being made here in English between wisdom in general, very much a human potentiality, and the *only* wisdom, here associated with the Logos as one of its qualities. The ambiguity being expressed points to the problem of human understanding of the Logos referred to in Fragment 1.

As part of the iconography of Greek religious experience, the name Zeus, together with his thunderbolt, expressed a range of meanings mostly associated with cause and effect in the physical realm and psychological motivation in the emotional or affective realm. Athena, symbol of Wisdom, was born directly from the head of her father Zeus, emerging, therefore, directly into wisdom from consciousness. These images helped to explain more expressively the order of body, mind, and soul in the abstract.

Fragment 8 expresses something of the mythological birth of Wisdom from Bright Consciousness: **Of all the accounts I have heard, not one rises to this: to know that wisdom is separate from all things.** Here, Heraclitus affirms the nature of Wisdom as being an entity not arising from Nature. We find this same affirmation in Plato, who separated wisdom from the other virtues and made its acquisition a matter of *anamnesis*, the remembrance of philosophic inquiry and discipline. The acquisition of wisdom is difficult and requires special prophetic intervention.

One point of contact from the divine to the human realms in the actual world-order took place in the sacred precinct belonging to Apollo at Delphi. As we have said, Apollo, the son of Zeus, was the Logos of Zeus. Apollo spoke the thoughts of Zeus through the oracle in the inner sanctum of the temple. For that reason Heraclitus was deliberate in including oracular truth in his philosophical vision. Fragment 51 describes the oracular nature: **The divine one whose oracle is in Delphi speaks neither directly or obscurely, but rather gives a sign.** The Logos was to be comprehended in the human realm through signs, ambiguous notes in the music of the spheres. Those foolish enough to assemble those notes into the songs they preferred to hear from the oracle paid the consequences, as history reveals time after time.

The Logos is comprehended in a manner closely resembling the oracular style of Delphi, as reflected in Fragment 52: **The raving Sibyl, through the god, utters somber, unembellished and unperfumed sayings, reaching over a thousand years with her voice.** The use of the image of the Sibyl reaches back prior to the temple of Apollo and the more formal organization of the Delphic system. The Sibyls of old perched on rocks and hurled their "ravings" with deep belly-roaring voices at those frightened mortals who dared to approach. Unlike the more refined atmosphere of the temple precinct, the Sibyls gave their messages unadorned with the priestly iambs quotable to kings or generals waiting for advice back home. Sibyls were always on the verge of madness in their trances, like instruments played upon by gods too huge and rough for the delicate frames singing at their command.

It is inescapable to conclude that in the Greek tradition the divine and human realms were so far apart in their nature that efforts to bridge the distance was always fraught with danger for humans and distortion for the gods.[17] The

---

17. In the *Tao Te Ching*, chapter five, we hear the following:
   The space between heaven and earth is like a bellows.
   The shape changes but not the form;
   The more it moves, the more it yields.
   More words count less.
   Hold fast to the center.

efforts of humans to approach the divine realm through ritual or ceremony were often met with either silence or vio-
lence. Only the great heroes braved the attempt at direct
assault on Olympus and were cheered on or condemned by
ordinary mortals for their excesses (*hybris*). When, in their
realm, the gods attempted to communicate, the results were
often misunderstood or ignored, leading to disaster and/or
death. The exception to this pattern occurred in Homeric
epic when the gods made sudden appearances in human
form to aid or obstruct mortals. Heraclitus abhorred these
characterizations and was reported in one of the more dubious fragments to have said, "Homer deserves to be stricken
from the lists and beaten."

Philosophy, and not traditional religion or myth, was the
solution to this problem of bridging the sacred distance. The
philosopher developed a language of approach to the divine
realm. It involved a reasoned, sacred crossing, using
acquired wisdom to discern divine messages from the
Beyond.

The Logos in the World Order

As we saw in his attitude towards Homer, Heraclitus was
critical of systems of thought that civilized the gods into patterns of good and evil or expressed a cosmos that was too
benign. Included in the order of the Logos were awesome
displays of raw power, but whatever the outcome or action,
it was nonetheless perfect.: **To God all things are beautiful,
good and just, but human beings have supposed some things
to be unjust, others just** (Fragment 13). Here is the fact of
human ignorance making its feeble efforts to explain, divide
and categorize. God must, we feel, love this and abhor that
because those are our cultural preferences and God must be
with us, on our side and against those others.

What can be the meaning of this fragment in the light of human experience? Injustice appears rampant; evil exists, not only at the demonic level, but at the depraved human level as well. Random accident and tragedies of all kinds cause untold suffering and despair, calling into serious question the "goodness" of God. From *evil* to *wicked* to *tragic*, we have no loss of words to describe our own version of the opposite of good and virtue in the world, and yet Heraclitus takes away this particular opposition where in other fragments he seems to declare that all things exist only through such opposition. Why?

In a world in which accident is common and suffering strikes the seeming innocent along with the seeming guilty, we have traditionally attributed divine agency as the cause. The earliest so-called nature religions developed rituals to assuage the anger of the spirits which controlled irrational occurrences, and if things turned out badly, the gods were flogged. Greek religion as well was predominantly concerned with divine intervention in the natural and human world. For Heraclitus to suggest that "all things" are beautiful, good and just" shattered ordinary preconceptions of divine control and intervention.

A Hindu parallel to Fragment 13 can be found in the Upanishads (literally 'at the feet of the master'). The Eesha Upanishad begins,

"That is perfect. This is perfect.
Perfect comes from perfect.
Take perfect from perfect, the remainder is perfect."[18]

The key to this famous sutra is in the translation of "That" and "This," the words referring to all worlds, much like the Greek sense of *ta panta*, or "all things." Although

---

18. *Ten Principle Upanishads*, trans. W.B. Yeats; Collier Books, New York, 1975.

individual human beings may indeed suffer, the cosmos itself is perfect. Nature is perfect in the sense of being what it is. The Eesha Upanishad continues:

"Whatever lives is full of the Lord. Claim nothing; enjoy, do not covet His property."[19]

Within this ultimate perfection, the "that" and "this" of *ta panta* is the active principle of opposition, the clash of forces out of which all things arise from the Logos. Our problem is that concepts of opposition, flux, tension, and movement have similar characteristics but different implications for the nature of reality, and we are not always able to make clear distinctions. Heraclitus expresses a vision of the Logos as resolving these oppositions, for example, in Fragment 9: **We have as One in us that which is living and dead, waking and sleeping, young and old: because these having transformed are those, and those having transformed are these.**

The Logos exists in us as a unity of forces in flux: life/death, waking/sleeping, youth/age. If **The way up and the way down are one and the same** (Fragment 7), then these transforming states exist in us simultaneously. It is not a matter of potential or alteration. I am alive in my death as I am dead in my life. I am awake in sleep because aspects of my brain are attentive and, certainly, asleep when awake in that aspects of my awareness are not functioning. For the Logos, time does not exist, and all things happen simultaneously, and are constantly in motion while yet remaining absolutely still.

These fragments help human understanding to penetrate the veil of reality directly to the Logos, to be where it emanates so as to know both its energy and its nature. The act of penetration passes through illusory planes of cause and

19. Ibid, p. 15.

effect to rest, finally, at the still point, a place of perfect tension. As always, Heraclitus is the instigator, making statements not only to reveal but also to shatter the old and establish new patterns of perception. In Fragment 10, which we have already seen as revealing the complexity of unity, we see as well the dynamics of the process of change and flux. All things change, is one idea. All things are in flux, is another. If things changing are also in flux, then the condition is totally fluid. The change is changing. Opposites are only momentarily in tension; they next become identical, as one thing becomes another before either can be identified as one thing or another. My joy contains sorrow even before its sweetness can be fully savored. It is not, therefore, merely that the seeds of sorrow are found in joy, but that each is the other at once in flux. What seems an oxymoron on the surface of expression is the reality beneath it.

If the more things change the more they remain the same, then the more things are in flux the more they are a unity. Fragment 11 moves us into this unity of flux by example from human experience: **God is day/night, winter/summer, war/peace, fullness/hunger; the experience of God changes in the way that wine, when it is mixed with spices, is named according to the scent of each.**

The reference to wine in the fragment is only a guess on the part of any translator, since whatever substance is mixed with spices is actually missing from the text.[20] The nature of God in human eyes changes (being willing and not willing to be called Zeus) as human understanding flavors the abstraction with tangible qualities. It is not that God is protean, changing form at will, but that human beings change their view of God according to their needs, taste, and perceptions.

---

20. The word fire *(pyre)* was supplied by Diels and accepted by more commentators. The idea is that various kinds of incense "flavor" fire and give different essences or effects. The word could also have been any neutral substance which is changed or flavored to produce different tastes.

This question of who or what does the changing and what is changed emerges in Fragments 21 and 22. In Fragment 21 different people step into the same river:

New and different waters flow around those who step into the same river. It disperses and comes together . . . flows in and out . . . towards us and away.

In Fragment 22 the river is eternally changing, never repeating and yet always flowing the same way. It *appears* always to be the same river. **[Heraclitus says somewhere that] all things are in process and nothing stays still, and [comparing all things to flowing waters, he says] we cannot step twice in the same river.**

Each individual's experience in the cosmos is as unique as the step into the river and yet the experience itself is universal, as the river is uniform for each individual who steps into its flow. The Logos is such a stream of energy, into which we step uniquely and yet uniformly as human beings. The importance of this dictum is that we are not the Logos ourselves, and yet we step into its energy, its flow, and use its energy for our actions. We are in it; it is not in us.

Problems of Definition

Defining an elusive word from another language and time is a challenging business. If we were able to see the word whole, somehow in four dimensions, including time (history), or were able to visualize it in all its contexts simultaneously, its full nature and sense might appear to us as an object floating in space. One possibility is to place the term within a symbolic construct, which, in its own frame of reference, amplifies the word in question.

An example of such a construct is the ancient tetractys, a Pythagorean icon symbolic of the cosmos, reflective of its essential harmony, and sacred among Egyptian and Greek esoteric sources. The tetractys is a way of illustrating the

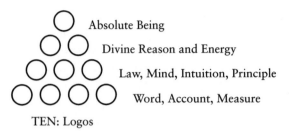

importance of the number ten as a key to various harmonies and a visual description of natural hierarchies. It appears as a pyramid of ten points, as follows:

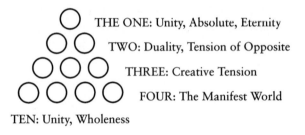

If we apply the word Logos to this pattern, placing its various translated meanings in the hierarchy, we may be able to imagine something of its connotation in Heraclitus.

The Logos Defined

We arrive, finally, at the idea and nature of the Logos through the fragments, first describing what it is not in the apophatic tradition, and then describing something in the affirmative of possible experience with it. First, what it is not:

It is not a god in any mythopoetic sense.

It is not solely a physical law like the law of gravity or thermodynamics.

It is not a system such as a solar system or a galaxy.

It is not a quality like love, although it possesses qualities.

It is not a spirit like some distinct disembodied entity.

It is not mind, although it is perceived through consciousness and is known to us through the reasoning faculty of the mind.

It is not fire, although it is manifest as fiery energy.

It is not the Abyss, in the sense of the void or emptiness.

Approached positively, the Logos can be described as emanating certain qualities and images which, although not identical to it, most approach its nature, something like giving it an environment in which it thrives or giving it qualities that emanate from it into manifestation.

The first image, which reflects the nature of the Logos as One and indivisible, is the unified field as expressed by modern physics. The primary qualities expressed by that concept are unlimitedness and timelessness, plus the notion of embracing all possibilities of manifestation. It is also causal in the sense that the physical universe would not and can not exist as it does without its presence and manifesting power. How the universe exists and that it exists at all is the direct result of its nature. Therefore, we experience the nature of the Logos when we accurately experience the world. We exist through it, because of it, and we take our sense of meaning from its qualities. Indeed, our longing for immortality is nothing more than the eternal nature of the Logos manifesting itself in our nature. Thus, true human nature is

Logos nature in microcosm. As we may some day know our-selves, we may also know the Logos.

The next important step identifies the Logos with unity, which for our purposes and perception is understood as the opposite of separation. We are free (and paradoxically at one with the Logos) when we perceive no separation from it in the context of our existence. This absence of separation is not necessarily connected to a specific feeling (such as bliss) or conscious perception, although a feeling akin to joy may well arise as a result of the perception of unity.

The Logos has its being (in a sense it "operates") in the space which is that absence of separation. In that so-called space (really more of a texture or dynamic) rests the poten-tial of creation and dissolution, both of which are cyclical and harmonious expressions of the Logos. Again, in positive terms, we can say that the opposite of separation is relation-ship, or connection. The Logos, then, connects us to divinity and to universal law. Insofar as we connect with another per-son, we anticipate and mimic the Logos in its nature and operations. Hence the marriage ceremony is a likeness and an icon.

Logos is also closely related to the noun "thought" and the verb "drive." In that sense, Fragment 34 comes closest to expressing a human understanding of Logos in expressing two of its crucial qualities. **To be wise is one thing: to know the thought that directs all things through all things,** describes the manifest Logos in human knowing, just as we understand the dynamics of ionization and movements of warm and cold air through the manifestation of lightning.

Denial of the Logos, that is, conscious separation from it, means that we are confined to an existence of individuality in which we are condemned to formulating our own systems and rules of existence. Such separation is the opposite of wis-dom and is hell on earth, as it were. The more we convince ourselves of the rightness of our separation, the more we remain alone and alienated, the more we confine ourselves to some private vision. As we shall see more clearly in the discussion of *ethos* or human nature, philosophical sleep leads to the isolating world of private visions.

The way of the Logos, on the other hand, allows us to fall freely into an intuitive self-forgetting in an act of absolute trust. It is stepping off the cliff of habitual existence into the "arms" of an invisible support. Whatever the imagery, whether self-forgetting or Logos-trust, the action is one of abandonment, particularly of one's idea of possession and/or ego identity. No sense of "mine" ever enters this space, only one of service, but without the attitude or sense of being the server. What we call *attitude* is always, whether it is positive or negative, pleasant or offensive, a separation from the flow of this Logos energy. Obedience to the flow is neutral. We act in it without attitude or commentary. We would never think of claiming to be swimming as we floated on our backs downstream.

In this discussion, the term "flow" refers to circumstances of time and space and can also be thought of as a context. Each context makes demands because a flow of power always exists towards something in a context. No context is without its demand because its nature in time and space must of necessity be either creative or destructive. Occasionally, in moments of deep meditation, for example, it is possible to become removed from context and become momentarily part of the stillness of the Logos-nature. Such moments are rare, of course.

It is not, however, exclusively in such deep meditational states that the Logos is available to us. The senses, particularly sight and hearing, are capable of apprehending knowledge of the Logos. Such knowledge has about it the Greek sense of *harmonia*, which some translate as "harmony" but others more accurately call "attunement." Attunement is an approximation of the Logos in experience. In such a state, no edges exist, no boundaries are visible, no sound is other or external, no thought arises to interrupt or displace the moment. How special, unique or "deep" the experience is matters less than one might suppose. Where we reside on the nexus of unity is less important than the fact of our presence in the neighborhood, on some level. Any degree is a gift; it is grace and is not to be overtly desired or sought after, and it is never possessed. To repeat: the Logos is not in us; we are in it. We are receivers of its emanations and transmitters of its signs.

PHYSIS

Physis is nature, understood broadly, and since we have some evidence that Heraclitus entitled his book "On Nature" and that he was regarded as a natural philosopher, it is fitting that we explore this term isolated from *logos*. Establishing credibility for his observations of a nature accessible to observation may lend greater credibility to his theological insights. Also, for the purposes of discussing various fragments, nature will be all that is not human, what lies outside human "nature," which we will consider later on under the term *Ethos*.

First, however, some background. The four major natural philosophers of Ionia, Thales, Anaximander, Anaximenes, and Xenophanes (the latter a contemporary of Heraclitus), are considered the major precursors of natural science in the West. Our contemporary attitude concerning their theories and general knowledge of the universe is generally controlled by our attitudes about the progress of human understanding over the millennia.

If, on the one hand, we feel that human beings have evolved substantially in their capacity to understand the world around them and have made genuine progress during the last two thousand years in understanding themselves and their world, then we tend to undervalue the contributions of the pre-Socratic natural philosophers, regarding their work as primitive. If, on the other, we hold that human beings have not evolved very much as a species in that time and that modern technology has blinded rather than extended their understanding into realms excessively rational, then we are inclined to exaggerate the insights of the pre-Socratics and credit them with extensive esoteric knowledge we do not possess.

The truth lies somewhere in between. Accuracy, as usual, lies both in the careful examination of the relevant evidence and in making sound, if intuitive, judgments about that evidence. Too often, the same biased commentators whose prejudices have influenced our knowledge of Heraclitus, have also influenced our knowledge of his contemporaries. The sources are the same.

The city-state of Miletus was located south of Ephesus along the coast of Asia Minor. It was home to three of the great sixth-century B.C. thinkers: Thales, Anaximander, and Anaximenes. What we know of Thales is that he predicted an eclipse in 585 B.C. and that his interests extended to mathematics and geometry. The Aristotelian commentator Simplicius (sixth century A.D.) had this to say about Thales: "Thales is traditionally the first to have revealed the investigation of nature to the Greeks; he had many predecessors, as also Theophrastus thinks, but so far surpassed them as to blot out all who came before him. He is said to have left nothing in the form of writings except the so-called 'Nautical Star-Guide.'"[21] Thus we are justified in beginning with Thales.

Since Simplicius is to be trusted in this opinion, we generally credit Thales with first breaking the mythopoetic hold on descriptions of cosmology and natural phenomena. His prediction of an eclipse means that he had much more than a rudimentary knowledge of astronomy. As to his investigations into the nature of matter, he is said to have regarded water as the fundamental element, although it may well be that he observed that water was the essential ingredient of life and so named it as essential to all of creation.

What we know and understand of Anaximander is more tantalizing than informative. His combination of abstract thinking and concrete observation, juxtaposed as they are so closely, give us a clue about the power of pre-Socratic thinking. These expansive geniuses moved easily from one level of

---

21. *The Presocratic Philosophers*, G. S. Kirk, J. E. Raven, M. Schofield; Cambridge University Press, Cambridge, 1983, p. 86.

consideration to another, combining, opening avenues of inquiry, stretching thinking itself into infinite realms. It is not the sort of thinking we are accustomed to encountering.

Anaximander developed the theory of the *apeiron*, a Greek term meaning "infinite" or "indefinite," depending on how we wish to apply it to cosmology and nature. He was able, I believe, to posit the concept of infinity as a measure of the cosmos, although we cannot be certain just how metaphysical his conception was or how far into the infinite his perception extended. Simplicius again provides the key description in saying that Anaximander posits ". . . some other *apeiron* nature, from which come into being all the heavens and the worlds in them. And the source of coming-to-be for existing things is that into which destruction, too, happens, according to Necessity; for they pay penalty and retribution to each other for their injustice according to the assessment of Time."[22]

Although the personification of matter in the idea of the payment of a penalty may strike us as too anthropomorphic and indicate the residue of mythic thinking, the image is nonetheless scientifically accurate. Changes in the state of matter do exact a (kind of) penalty owed to the power of necessity residing within the principle of the conservation of matter. The "injustice" involved has to do with the expenditure of energy in the form of heat or the loss of speed because of friction or the cost in heat and energy in order to create or fly or find food. Nature is absolutely just in this regard, totally "just" in its requirements. There is no free lunch in nature. This observation, combined as it is with the more metaphysical observation of the way in which the *apeiron* in its infinite wisdom and nature dictates or directs this justice is a theme which Heraclitus develops more fully.

---

22. Ibid. p. 118.

The Roman commentator Augustinius relates the following: "Anaximander thought that things were born not from one substance, as Thales thought from water, but each from its own particular principles. He believed these principles to be infinite, giving birth to endless worlds . . . and these worlds are dissolved, are born again, according to the limits each was able to survive." Here, too, we find echoes of Heraclitus and a refinement of the principles of how the cosmos does, in fact, operate.

The other fragments extant from Anaximander offer similar hints of the sophistication of his cosmology. He posited, for example, that the earth was a cylinder supported by the air and in one fragment said, "The earth is on high, held up by nothing, but remaining on account of its similar distance from all things."[23]

Anaximenes was also from Miletus and was, we assume, the pupil of Anaximander. His contribution to the knowledge of *physis* was to refine the notions of both Thales and his teacher and to approach an understanding of how matter is created. Although not an atomist, he did intuit how the One became All Things. According to Hippolytus, "Anaximenes . . . says that the underlying nature is one and infinite, but not undefined as Anaximander said but definite, for he identifies it as air; and it differs in its substantial nature by rarity and density. Being made finer it becomes fire, being made thicker it becomes wind, then cloud, then (when thickened still more) water, then earth, then stones; and the rest come into being from these. He, too, makes motion eternal, and says that change, also, comes about through it."[24]

Heraclitus refined this observation, coming closer to the truth not so much through changing the prescription but

---

23. Ibid. p. 134.
24. Ibid. p. 145.

through his use of language. His syntax leaves more room for detail to be filled in later, almost as if he understood intuitively that more would need to be learned through means not at his disposal.

The last of the precursors of Heraclitus was Xenophanes, who spent his early years in Kolophon, just north of Ephesus. He, too, was an expatriate, having been banished from Kolophon, presumably for his radical religious views. His views on nature, however, were critical to the growing awareness of the Earth's formation. Hippolytus provides the following important data: "Xenophanes thinks that a mixture of the earth with the sea is going on, and that in time the earth is dissolved by the moist. He says that he has demonstrations of the following kind: shells are found inland and in the mountains, and in the quarries in Syracuse he says that an impression of a fish and of seaweed has been found." Others, we must assume, also found fossils and shells left from the more recent ice age, but Xenophanes made systematic observations and drew general conclusions from them, illustrating Heraclitus' observation that real perception comes from those things which yield themselves to sight and hearing.

We begin a consideration of a Heraclitean vision of nature with Fragment 15: **Nature prefers to hide**. The lines of code are buried. The particles defy analysis. They operate randomly and yet obey hidden laws. In 500 B.C., however, Heraclitus drew his understanding from principles of attunement, opposition, change, and transformation, all of which are qualities as much as phenomena. All things are in process and nothing stays still.

In settling on fire as fundamental to nature, Heraclitus was betting on transformation as the fundamental principle underlying coming-to-be and the diversity of nature. His own experiments with fire, steam, dissolving matter, and physical exchange, gave him the clues to offer fire as the symbol of creation and dissolution.

In the biographical reference about the stove, Heraclitus said, "Do not fear, the gods are here also." We asked earlier why students would fear to enter a room merely because Heraclitus was standing by the stove, unless, of course, he was doing something at the stove that caused them to be afraid, or hesitant, at least.

That Heraclitus experimented with the phenomenon of fire and its properties seems certain. Whether or not this fact makes him an alchemist, in the Late medieval sense of that term, is questionable. We do know, for example, that Marsilio Ficino, whose influence upon Renaissance thought is seminal, devoted his considerable talents to alchemy as well as to the translation and interpretation of ancient Greek and Roman texts and that in his essay "Liber de Arte Chemica," he expands on the relation of fire to nature and has Heraclitus and the Logos in mind as he does so. Here is Ficino on Heraclitus:

> Nature is therefore a certain invisible fire, by which Zoroaster taught that all things were begotten, to whom Heraclitus the Ephesian seems to give consent. Did not the spirit of the Lord, which is a fiery love, when it was carried on the waters, put into them a certain fiery vigor? Since nothing can be generated without heat. God inspired into created things, when it was said in the generation of the world, increase and be ye multiplied, a certain germination, that is, a greenness, by which all things might multiply themselves. Whence some more profoundly speculative, said that all things were green, is called to grow and increase, and that greenness they named Nature.[25]

---

25. Transcribed by Justin von Budjoss. This text is a translation of a Latin text, Marsilius Ficinus, "Liber de Arte Chemica," which was printed in the *Theatrum Chemicum*, vol 2, Geneva, 1702, p. 172-183.

Heraclitus understood the transformational qualities of fire and devoted considerable space in his book to observations of its effects and qualities. That "The lightning directs everything" should be his calling card, as it were, tells us a great deal about his devotion to fire as an image of the cosmos and the cause of the "greenness" of nature.

Heraclitus attracted students eager to penetrate the surfaces of the manifest world to comprehend it and then to seek transformation to a higher knowledge of the cosmos. The fragments we will examine in this regard place him at least marginally among those who experimented with physical and/or chemical processes as part of the transformational purpose of human *ethos*.

We can turn now to the fragments most concerned with this theme. The first and most challenging is Fragment 25: **Fire's alternations: first as sea, and of sea half earth and half lightning dispersed as sea, and measured in the same proportion as existed before it became earth.** Heraclitus knew well, as we have said, the debt nature owes the sun. Not only cycles of wind, rain, evaporation, clouds — the whole cycle of natural growth and seasons — but very existence itself. Since everything alive is generated by the sun, nothing would exist without its radiant heat. Our very civilization is a product of the sun, in every aspect. The "fire" that generates life also generates thought in the human organism.

Our fire-thought emulates the Logos-fire of the cosmos, indeed is an echo of it in form. To know human consciousness is to have access to the Logos, just as an icon mimics the Idea in symbolic proportion. Number and geometry mimic the eternal forms in the same way. The Pythagoreans turned this idea on its head by supposing that Number was the ultimate Form rather than its symbol or icon. We possess knowledge of the unfathomable through number and geometry. We know the Logos through the manifestations of fire in the cosmos. And most important, we know ourselves and the nature of the transformations we pass through because we can also know the same transmutations of the four elements: fire, water, earth and air in their transit through nature.

In the more contemporary alchemical world of scientific experimentation on the origins of life, scientists beginning in the 1950s created in the laboratory the conditions that may have existed several billion years ago when life on Earth began. The chemical soup they mixed in flasks was fired both with heat and with electric charges in an attempt to mimic the impact on likely chemical mixtures struck by lightning. Their assumption was that the complex leap to living organisms from organic chemistry needed the power (or the direction) of lightning. The result of this experimentation was the creation of amino acids, the building blocks of living systems.

Heraclitus could not have managed experimentation with lightning, nor was it his intention to create life, as far as we know. Any experimentation for him must have focused on chemical combining under the influence of moderate heat, with evaporation and condensation as two phenomena worthy of study. The general concerns of alchemical experimentation in this early period would have centered on metallurgy and understanding the nature of humors in the psychic and physiological realms. The brief chapter entitled "Humours" in the works of Hippocrates, differs from the rest of the Hippocratic corpus in being both more ancient and more enigmatic.[26]

The focus of his brief collection of aphorisms is systemic balance and the extremes of ill health based on bodily fluids, excretions, dryness, colors, and seasonal change. The history of this collection suggests ancient sources for many of its observations and extensive experimentation by later practitioners. Heraclitus was more interested in nature than he

---

26. *Hippocrates*, vol. iv, trans. W .H. S. Jones, Harvard University Press, Cambridge, 1931

was in human physiology. The fragments concern themselves more with the humours of the earth and its various transmutations. Antoine Faivre describes these concerns in his study, *Access to Western Esotericism*,

> Nature occupies an essential place. Multilayered, rich in potential revelations of every kind, it must be read like a book. The word *magia*, so important in the Renaissance imaginary, truly calls forth that idea of Nature, seen, known, and experienced as essentially alive in all its parts, often inhabited and traversed by a light or a hidden fire circulating through it. [27]

This vision expresses well the way Heraclitus examined nature and drew from its secrets the essentials of his metaphysics. In the modern era, science separated nature from its divine ground in every respect. On the other hand, Heraclitus examined both himself and nature with a balanced eye, seeing the same principles in operation and seeing the same vital sources of energy and consciousness in both aspects of the cosmos. Modern reductive philosophy has placed human beings on the same low platform with their perception of the manifest world, seeing less there than actually exists. When Heraclitus took issue with the scientific explorations of Pythagoras and Hesiod, he was objecting to the same reductive analysis with the same reductive results.

The exercise in extrapolating viable information from doubtful and fragmentary sources has been admirably preceded by scholars and followers of Pythagoras. From the Neoplatonists onward we have ample treatments of the Pythagorean corpus, interpreted by esoteric thinkers to form a coherent and systematic "ism." We could almost reconstitute the operations of his school from the esoteric research

---

27. Antoine Faivre, *Access To Western Esotericism*, State University of New York Press, Albany, 1994, p. 276.

done over the course of two millennia. In the case of Heraclitus, however, we have no such extrapolated detail. What we do have is a method of approach and a syntax of inquiry.

In a real sense, what we have in the fragments forms a narrow, sometimes obliterated path through the wilderness of ancient thought. With Pythagoras, a portion of his particular path was opened into a clearing, or a system, or school, if you will. Subsequent thinkers (or seekers) found comfort in this clearing and remained there, building structures to provide metaphysical comfort and security. What they failed to see in their comfort and isolation is that the path continues out the other side of the clearing. The clearing is not a destination. Given their disastrous efforts to influence practical politics, however, we can hardly blame them for settling there.

Heraclitus, the pathfinder without clearings, studied both himself and the world. He used images from nature, including the elements of fire, water, earth and air, to formulate the nature of matter in relation to the Logos. Human beings, too, were manifestations of natural processes and were also infused with the Logos, although our senses had long since overwhelmed the subtle messages of the Logos and mired us in a banal existence to the detriment of our true nature.

The fire of the Sun begins all life as we know it.[28] The transformative cycles of water and earth and air take their form from fire, the first element. If we bring this knowledge to our own consciousness, making experience existential in other words, we free ourselves from the domination of ordinary cycles of experience in the fire of consciousness. So much of our lives is the pattern of eating, working, and

---

28. There is, of course, some debate about the role of the sun in the formation of life. Some now propose that life may have begun in volcanic fissures in the depths of the sea, without the benefit of sunlight. Nonetheless, the sun is still regarded as the generative source of all living things.

sleeping that we fail to "see" anything about the reality in which we have our being. The transformations of fire, in the form of the burning of energy from food, the transformations of calories to thought and creative power, the transformations of insight and awareness to fundamental changes in perception, all these are much more central to our existence than the content of any given day. Our constant fault is that we are not obedient to the call of the imagination as a force of pure fire. We fail to trust its transformative powers.

The faculty of human understanding tends to the literal. The constant challenge of text — or the Logos of human nature — is to seek out the transformational implications of language and syntax. There is a story about Heraclitus that illustrates the point. One commentary suggests that Heraclitus "believed" that the sun is in actuality the size that it appears to be. This erroneous conclusion was based on a comment he is purported to have made to the effect that the sun was the size of the width of a man's foot. Well, let us for the sake of the esoteric discussion, grant that Heraclitus might well have made such a statement. What might the context have been?

First, we have to know the "spirit" in which he may have made the statement. Only that context matters. The literal content is insignificant. He was certainly too intelligent not to understand the basic principle of apparent object size in relation to distance and thus not to know that the sun had to be very large and thus some great distance from the earth, although exactly how far, he had no idea. And yet, it is attributed to him to have said that the Sun was the width of a man's foot. It is not difficult to imagine Heraclitus seated among his students discussing the transformative power of fire as manifest in the Sun, only to have a student ask him, "How large is the Sun, master?" In response, and at the same level of the content, the master holds up a foot to shield his eyes from the glare and replies, "As wide as a man's foot. Now, where were we?" One hopes that the student, having asked an irrelevant question, would have taken the admonishment in stride and let the relevant discussion continue.

These are Socratic moments, elements of the dialectic of philosophical inquiry. Again, the content is not important. It is the insight that matters. It is not *what* we are thinking; it is *how* we are thinking and how we are listening. And, also critical to the esoteric purpose, it is in what *spirit* we are doing the work. If a student were foolish enough to part from Heraclitus thinking that the master actually assumed the Sun to be no bigger than the width of the foot that was shielding its light, then so be it. He left in ignorance. It is the same approach we find in the allegorical teachings of Jesus. If a disciple thought the subject of a parable was indeed seeds, for example, then we have to say that the disciple was one of the rocks onto which seeds occasionally fall and remain ungerminated.

Getting back to Fragment 25, **Fire's alternations: first as sea, and of sea half earth and half lightning dispersed as sea, and measured in the same proportion as existed before it became earth,** this time in a more analytical mode, we have been given in it a formula for what Heraclitus calls "alternations." The Greek is *tropai* and means "turning" and "change." It is often used in reference to the changes in natural cycles, such as when the seasons change. Seen in greater depth, however, we can also detect a pattern of alternation leaning to the transformational. Just as human beings are made of earth, water and air, into which the fire of life is breathed by the miracle of birth, so too we must see that the fact of our life is in itself a transformation of fire into the elements of our living or biological being. During the time we inhabit our bodies, we go through the same cyclical pattern of transformation as does the planet in its biosphere. As our biological life proceeds, we literally burn up the earth and water of our being until we become air and fire once again.

Physics tells us, for example, that we are mostly space and that seeming solidity is only an illusion. The molecules of our body are made up of atoms, which in turn are mostly space and very little matter. We have an illusion of solid matter only because of the strong, weak, and electro-magnetic forces holding atomic structure in place. As such, all solidity is an illusion. Heraclitus intuited both this structure and the flux inherent in it. His ambiguity is an expression of this knowledge.

Fragment 26 describes another feature of the transformations of fire. **All things equally exchange for fire as does fire for all things, as goods are exchanged for gold and gold for goods.** The analogy to gold draws attention to later alchemical themes but reflects in Heraclitus the concern for purity in the transformational exchange. This fragment establishes the primacy of fire as the *metron* or measure of "all things." *Ta panta,* the "all things" which signify the manifest world in its multiplicity, leads us to the fundamental unity of the cosmos, with fire as the controlling or directing element of that unity. The Logos demands that the exchange occur with balance, a preservation of matter and energy that guarantees a continual cycle of "arising and subsiding in measure," as expressed in Fragment 24. As such **This cosmos, [the unity of all that is] . . . is and will be an eternal fire . . . .** In the light of current cosmology, it is certainly not difficult to connect these intuitive constructs to the theories of the Big Bang and the fluctuating universe(s) of our current understanding. What takes us beyond the cosmology into the metaphysical is the constant connecting of language to human life, such as in Fragments 36, 37, and 41. In these fragments, we are meant to apply the lessons of careful observation of nature's cycles to human existence and being.

As we see in Fragment 36, **It is death for souls to become water.** In the work of esoteric transformation, the task is to expend the gross aspects of ourselves, to exhaust our resources like a candle, down to nothing. A dry soul can rise, escape the moist remains of the body, hence Fragment 37: **A dry soul is wisest and best.** We are literally to burn ourselves out. A moist soul, one confined to a "drunken" body, has no hope of release. Heraclitus did not believe that every soul made its way to a higher realm or plane. In the symbolic, or alchemical account of his life, we hear of him wandering in the mountains eating herbs. This symbolism places him at high altitude confining himself to food which barely sustains him. In nature, like flows to like, as like clings to like. Transformation releases a form to a new level or "likeness." Where does a candle "go" when it burns? Where does the flame "go" when it is extinguished? It doesn't just "go out." Some of the heat dissipates upwards, some molecules are absorbed into the surrounding air, and some molecules fall to the surface below as soot. Like to like.

In Fragment 41, another theme emerges to take us to another, more subtle level. The element of air fuels the fire that sets life in motion. We breathe in the sustaining oxygen that is transformed into life-giving energy. That Heraclitus refers to this process as "drawing in the Logos" connects the life-giving air with the law-giving substance of the Logos. There is knowledge in the air we breathe. When we inhale, we take in knowledge emanating from the Logos. When we exhale, we surrender to its truth and signal our obedience. We also transmit when we exhale our words. Knowing in, articulation out. In the meantime, our minds, if they are awake and alert, look out through the windows of perception and gather the power of Reason. It is this power which allows us to retain in memory the knowledge we breathe in and to exhale gratefully to the Logos.

The founding text of alchemic studies is the so-called
Emerald Table or Tablet. It is found in the Hermeticum and
has always been attributed to the mythical Hermes Tris-
megistus. This translation is an English translation from the
version done by Jacques de Nuisement published originally
in 1621:

True it is; know with sure admiration
That the high is the same thing as the low
From all to one through one to all must go
All wondrous effects of adaptation.

One is turned to all through meditation,
As nurse and womb and parents it shall know
Earth the wind Diana and Apollo
In this thing alone lies all perfection.

Changed into earth its power is entire:
Gently separate the earth from the fire.
The subtle with great wisdom from the course.

From the earth it climbs to Heaven then to aspire
To earth once more where it will gain the force
Of each the high and low that all require.[29]

So many images and formulations in this famous text
coincide with the fragments of Heraclitus that we must conclude that the later Hermetic writers must have had the
Heraclitus book in their possession and drew upon it. And,
too, we have to wonder why the fragments have not captured the closer attention of serious alchemists, that is, of

---

29. Antoine Faivre, *Access to Western Esotericism.* State University of New
York Press, Albany. 1994, p. 171.

those whose philosophical interests run parallel to their physical investigations.

Finally, nature for Heraclitus was alive, full of gods, transformative in its essence and very real. It was not Other or seen as illusion, as it would become to Plato and the Neoplatonists. Even though Heraclitus could say, as he did in Fragment 31, **It makes more sense to throw out a corpse than manure,** he did not dismiss nature as dead matter or seek to deny sensory knowledge. Nature is the expression of the Logos, as are human beings, and our task is to wake up and participate consciously.

Nomos

In the world of *physis,* of fire, earth, air, and water, the Logos manifests itself as *nomos*, the Law. In Kathleen Freeman's translations of the fragments, the word *logos* often appears in English as Law. The difficulty of this choice becomes apparent when the word *nomos* (law as well as custom) also appears. Freeman makes a parenthetical distinction, calling Logos the law "of the universe" and *nomos* "political law." For the bulk of Greek literature and philosophy the choice of "political law" for *nomos* is sufficient, but with Heraclitus difficulties arise. The relation of *logos* to *nomos* is close, to be sure, in that the Logos is that conscious harmony or attunement of the created universe, which certainly manifests itself as being lawful, and *nomos* in its philosophical sense carries (or should carry) a similar meaning, particularly as it relates to *physis*.

As is evident from the historical record, however, the political laws enacted by human beings do not often correspond to either the Logos or *physis*. For the most part the *nomoi* fall into the category of rules. When Heraclitus abdicated his patrimony and refused to write laws (*nomoi*) for Ephesus on the grounds that the city was already too corrupt and was thus beyond salvation, he spoke of the *nomoi* in very different terms from mere political or written laws. His concerns were to establish *nomoi* that would be consistent with the Logos and *physis* and would embody the principles of his highest ideals.

The primary fragment concerned with his ideals of *nomos* is Fragment 57. **Those who speak with sense rely on what is universal, as a city must rely on its law, and with much greater reliance. For all man-made laws are nourished by one divine law; for it [Logos] has as much power as it wishes and is sufficient for all with more left over.** Here Heraclitus establishes

the fundamental relation between the Logos and political law-
making. We are accustomed to hearing kings and political philosophers making the connection between God's will and
political order. The laws of theocratic regimes such as the current one in Iran, attest to this struggle to apply sacred principle to political order, more often than not with an oppressive
impact on individual rights.

Heraclitus, however, makes a different point. This fragment suggests that a city's *nomoi* must be properly nourished
by the Logos. As such, the test of a city's laws are the extent
to which they are sustained by their application and remain
vital (nourished) by principle. If a law is oppressive, if it fails
to nourish the culture and those who must be obedient to it,
then it is not universally sound. The Logos has infinite power
to nourish and sustain human culture. It possesses unlimited
resources. If a city exhibits signs of atrophy or declines in its
vitality, then it must look to its laws and, more to the point,
to the source of its laws.

Without overtly saying so in any of the fragments, Heraclitus implies that the role of lawmaker must belong to a philosopher-king, as later proposed by Plato. It cannot be the
Many, or the people in this case, who make the laws, since
the laws arise from the Logos and are thus universally
founded. Why then, we ask, did Heraclitus refuse the role of
the city's lawgiver? Why not undertake the task Solon
accepted for Athens? Was Heraclitus so much the misanthrope that he could not bring himself to assume such a role?
The answer may lie with his friend Hermodorus, who was
banished by the Ephesians, who said, "We will have none
who is worthiest among us; or if there be any such let him go
elsewhere and consort with others."

Fragment 58 affirms this point of view. **It is also lawful to
obey the will of one man.** We would add "if he is the best"
from Fragment 60: **For me, one man is worth ten thousand**

others if he is the best. The principle of the Platonic philosopher-king has its foundation in fragments of this stamp. As we look back on 2,500 years of experimentation in the variety of political order, we understand the difficulty of implementing an order based on a dimly perceived Logos. Certainly Mosaic law makes the attempt. God speaks the Logos to Moses in the form of ten laws, which express its lawful principles. The people, however, cannot function effectively with just ten laws. They have no foundation which would permit them to expand the ten into a viable social order. Instead, society founders on the rocks of minute rules and regulations that seek to control every aspect of human life in the name of sacred law.

Effective political order, as we experience it, is democratically based upon the principle of the social contract. Individuals agree to surrender certain freedoms and rights in order to achieve and maintain an orderly society. The resulting system is inevitably flawed, but it works well enough. Clearly the leaders of Ephesus, in coming to Heraclitus to seek his wise counsel, were not interested in the Logos. They wanted a body of rules and regulations, and Heraclitus was not interested in complying with their request. Why?

What we have in Heraclitus is an order of human life not reflected in culture. When he abandoned the *polis* to its inevitable chaos and corruption, he selected instead the monodrama of the individually examined life that is nonetheless universal in its origins and articulation. In other words, he thought cosmically and acted individually. It is in that sense that the fragments are to be absorbed. His followers had to work hard to find in his teaching, of which the fragments are signposts or indications, the core of a way of life. Certainly Heraclitus was not a democrat. He was, however, a libertarian in the sense of his demand that he be free from the restraints of government in his explorations and his expression of their results. In effect, he chose to live "off the grid" as it were. In that sense he was quite different from Socrates.

One can only imagine that in a polis where Heraclitus was king *(basileus)*, very little restriction would be placed on individual expression, but that corruption would be severely punished. The *nomoi,* or man-made laws, would be a reflection of the Logos, emphasizing individual freedom to realize oneself in an atmosphere of guided personal inquiry. At the same time, a system of laws based upon the Logos would be severely just, meaning that expectations for acting in accordance with the best aspirations of the culture would be strictly enforced. The laws *(nomoi)* would be based on the principle of *palintropos,* or opposed coherence leading to a fine attunement.

Such *nomoi* are not only related to the Logos, but are also tied closely in principle to *physis*, nature. Following Heraclitus in the Greek fifth century B.C., the great Athenian writers of tragedy, Aeschylus, Sophocles, and Euripides, employed the mythopoetic drama of the gods entwined in the lives of human beings to confront the great themes of the age: suffering, heroism, love, justice, law, and the meaning of life. They also framed their plays in the tensions between great principles: word versus deed (*logos* versus *ergon)* and nature versus law (*physis* versus *nomos*). It is a certainty that the three great tragedians, whose thirty-three extant works remain to us, were students of philosophy and that they thought and wrote on the grandest scale about the great intellectual issues of the day.

As noted above it is told with a certain understandable awe that one day Euripides gave a copy of Heraclitus' book to Socrates, who admired it and commented on its complexity and obscurity. We do not know, however, what the great Euripides himself thought about it, except what we are able to deduce from the extant plays. One would suppose that if he offered a copy of Heraclitus to Socrates, that Euripides was not merely passing it on, but that he admired the book and that he drew upon its themes for his own use. We know, for example, that Euripides was an irascible sort and might well have found in Heraclitus a soul mate. We also know from the nineteen extant plays of Euripides that human nature (*ethos*) was often controlled by a guiding daemon of destructive power over which the individual had little or no control. The fundamental pessimism ruling the drama of Euripides has a certain Heraclitean cast. One might suppose that Heraclitus would have applauded Medea, for example.

Euripides' philosophical interests might have focused upon the searing criticism of contemporary Athenian society evidenced in the plays. He was more interested in the conflict between individuals, with the resulting dislocations of myth versus law and cultural values. The law of coherent opposition, so crucial to an understanding of reality in Heraclitus, was dramatized by Euripides in the conflicts between Pentheus and Dionysus, Admetus and Alcestis, Hippolytus and Pheadra, and most famously, Jason and Medea. The result was always a terrifying justice, often too overwhelming to behold. But always there resulted in the formation of new *nomoi,* often of a transcendental nature.

In Sophocles, on the other hand, the tension of opposites manifested itself in the inner life of the individual, whose suffering in the world brought about a transformation of inner sight and a new awareness or self-knowledge. We see this theme in Ajax, Antigone, Philoctetes, Electra and of course, Oedipus. All of these figures emerged from their personal suffering at the hands of *nomoi* imposed upon their *physis* or "nature." Their sense of honor (based on *physis)* was shattered by arbitrary laws imposed by cultural expediency and personal greed. In Sophocles, the figures of Creon and Odysseus are representatives of these corrupting *nomoi.*

It is traditionally thought that Sophocles was a religious poet, that he was writing in order to affirm traditional religious values in a culture in which the State religion wished to impose its values upon the culture. Sophocles was, actually, a spiritual poet. His interest was in exploring the process by which suffering is able to transform the hero and as a direct result transform the values (*nomoi*) of the polis. Central to this transformation was the relation between the *nomoi* of the culture and the nature, or essence (*physis*), which was also a mirror of the Logos.

It is in this latter sense that we briefly turn to Sophocles to examine the role of *nomos* in Greek culture. In the *Antigone* we find the classic tension between conflicting *nomoi*. Antigone bases her existence and the meaning of her life on upholding the sacred laws of burial (the true *nomoi*), which her uncle Creon has countermanded for political expediency. His law is based on what he calls political necessity, hers on sacred tradition. In addition, Antigone bases her claim of efficacy on the relation of sacred law to natural law (*physis*). Her brother Polyneices lies dead, unmourned and unburied on the battlefield where he was slain. His brother Eteocles, also slain, is given a hero's burial by Creon, who wishes to demonstrate to the battered *polis* the rewards of loyalty and the price of treason. In giving burial to Polyneices, Antigone affirms her devotion to sacred law. Creon, on the other hand, in denying sacred law dooms himself and his family to just suffering.

But this tension of natural versus expedient law in dramatic form spells out a theme within the confines of the polis. Creon is the typical man of expediency who makes bad plans and as a result ends badly. He does not listen to the demands of nature and does not give proper attention to Delphic prophecy and other sane advice, such as the pleas from his son Haemon to change his mind and follow a different path. Instead he exhibits a stubborn adherence to his own private judgment. In this sense he is an example of those who possess only a **"private understanding,"** as we see expressed in Fragment 2. He leaves a body to rot in the sun, exposed to the light of day, and he confines Antigone, who embodies natural law, to a cave, to the darkness, there to die by her own hand. The dramatic symbolism is reflected in Fragment 46: **Immortal mortals, mortal immortals, living their death and dying their life.**

So too with all the Sophoclean heroes. The theme of the dislocation of law from nature, or life from Logos is reflected within the individual as much as within the *polis*. Heraclitus backed away from the corruption of Ephesus in order to find the Logos within himself. He discovered in the process that human nature *(ethos)* was cut off from nature *(physis)* and the Logos, and that the nomoi of human life made it impossible to recover. His choice to become a hermit, to repel any and every attempt of his culture to participate in its daily life, was not a matter of misanthropy. Rather, it was a philosophical necessity.

For example, we might look again, in the light of Sophocles, at the first two fragments. **1. The Logos, which is as I describe, proves incomprehensible, both before it is heard and even after it is heard. For although all things happen according to the Logos, many act as if they have no experience of it, even when they do experience such words and action as I explain, as when I separate out each thing according to its nature and state how it is; but as to the rest, they fail to notice what they do after they wake up, just as they forget what they do when they sleep.** And the next: **2. It is necessary, therefore, to obey the universal; but although the Logos is universal, most people live as though they had a private understanding.**

Does the ignorance of personal fate as exhibited by Creon in *Antigone* or Oedipus in *Oedipus the King* reflect the kind of ignorance expressed here? The answer is: only partially. The difference is that Heraclitus is speaking not solely of behavioral blindness or a weakness of character.

Rather, he is serving notice from a lifetime of seeking and discipline that he has awakened from the sleep of the ignorant to a new state of awareness and in that state he has new sight and new knowledge. And he is saying that it is possible, although difficult, for others to do the same.

By contrast, Creon and Oedipus lack wisdom, *sophia*, which is a virtue born of suffering, remembrance and insight. The result of their blindness is catastrophic, both to themselves and to the *polis*. We are able to see, then, particularly when we apply the fragments to the conflicts found in the plays, that wisdom (*sophia*) comes from the individual's painful and arduous journey to the Logos, in the process finding the true relation between Nature (*physis*) and the Law.

Another meaning of *nomos* in Greek culture's convention, common practice, and by extension, habit. Heraclitus applies that meaning to spiritual sleep, the banal existence of everyday life and empty behavior, both deadly to the spirit. When in Fragment 2, we hear that **Most people live as though they had a private understanding** we encounter the sense of *nomos* as indicative of that private world of sleep in which we exist but without the nourishment of the Logos.

The relationship between the *nomoi* of common practice and the concept of justice is expressed in Fragment 13: **To God all things are beautiful, good and just, but human beings have supposed some things to be unjust, others just.** Common usage renders certain actions good and others evil. Our hurried tendency to label things good and bad eventually create *nomoi,* which in turn become the habits or customs by which we live. These habits of attitude and action become common practice which becomes in turn lawful behavior, any breach of which is treated with harsh penalties. Fear of those penalties keeps us bound to the practices. Many spiritual disciplines, particularly those in the Buddhist tradition, are designed to break down these habits.

Fragment 13 also suggests that human beings base their sense of justice and the laws which maintain that justice, on personal considerations such as self-preservation and personal security. Since we know — or at least have heard — that in order to save our life we have to lose it, the way up being the way down, then our understanding of *nomos* must correspond to our understanding of the Logos. They are one and the same.

Thus it is that the fragments serve two simultaneous ends: to break down the habitual and static definitions of Logos, *nomos*, and *physis* and to establish their abiding relationship as principles arising from the same eternal and unquenchable source. The true test of any culture's *nomoi*, from the mundane stop sign to the sublime principle of free speech, lies in their abiding vitality. For Heraclitus those *nomoi* must reflect as well as serve the spiritual evolution (or becoming) of *ethos*, the essence of human nature.

ETHOS

The most challenging of the Heraclitean fragments to render into English is number 54: *ethos anthropoi daimon.* Most commentators simply translate "Character is fate." Kirk and Raven, aware of the ambiguities involved, intentionally leave *daimon* untranslated because of the serious philosophical problems involved in attempting an English equivalent such as "fate" or "destiny," which in turn proclaim a reductive meaning. Most other translators, those perhaps less concerned with philosophical issues and more with rendering the Greek into some brief form, just let the philosophical chips fall. Such is the case with Jones, Freeman and Burnet.

The authoritative Liddell and Scott Greek/English dictionary also chooses to place the fragment in a range of meanings closest to "the good or evil genius of a person," which settles on the Greek sense of *daimon* as a power influencing or even controlling human destiny. Wheelwright's translation, "A man's character is his guardian divinity,"[30] introduces the element of guidance or protection rather than control and, at the same time, opens the fragment to its full range of possibilities. But it isn't quite right.

The problem with "Character is fate" as the translation is that in both denotation and connotation no sense of the word *daimon* as spirit or some power either within or without is even implied, unless one wishes to burden the word "fate" with excessive determinism. Modern readers, however, feeling free of ruling forces (except the power of DNA, perhaps) understand such a translation to say that as human beings we hold our destiny in our own hands solely by virtue of our character. If, for example, I have an addictive person-

---

30. Philip Wheelwright, *Heraclitus*, Princeton University Press, Princeton, 1959, p. 68.

ality, I am liable to get into trouble with addiction. If, on the other hand, I have the strength of will to restrain myself from dangerous temptations, I will remain free of addiction and, one assumes, thought of as having a good or strong character. In that sense we limit the definition of "character" in ways not intended by Heraclitus.

If we consider a translation derived from the Liddell/Scott placement of the fragment, we would have to say either that a man's character is directed by his indwelling "genius," where genius refers to a tendency of intellect or of character or even personality, or that an indwelling "spirit" of some sort rules our actions, in spite of our intentions. In the latter case we cannot avoid the implication that human life is somehow determined, if not Calvinistically predetermined, then at least by the will of the gods or by some demonic power intent on exercising its control. Such is the context in which Heraclitus created his sentence. Homer, whose mythus was the guiding paradigm of the culture in which Heraclitus lived, described human destiny as being closely guided and/or controlled by demonic powers, including, of course, the Olympian gods.

Heraclitus, on the other hand, bases human nature within the protective domain of a more benevolent and benign Logos as well as in the potential power of human understanding and insight. We recall Fragment 13: **To God all things are beautiful, good and just, but human beings have supposed some things to be unjust, others just.** This certainly does suggest, then, that our destiny is determined by our ability to exercise the power we innately possess to discriminate between God's justice and our own flawed, vain opinions. It is this basis of human nature that is not reflected in translating *daimon* strictly as "destiny." We hold our lives in our own hands insofar as our constitution controls our choices and attitudes.

In Wheelwright's translation, the choice of stating directly that character is our guardian divinity suggests that it is character alone that guides us, somewhat like a guardian angel, but obviously not in such a detached presence. In this case, it is as if someone asked Heraclitus what or who guides our lives, and his answer was, "Character." On the surface, this choice is acceptable. Heraclitus answers the question with the word *ethos*. But as in many philosophical cases, this answer is correct only insofar as we can successfully translate *ethos*.

Some helpful light is shed on this problem by the unique work of Eric Voegelin (1901-1985), the author of the five volume *Order and History*, volume two of which is entitled *The World of the Polis* and covers in great depth the period of Heraclitus' activity. It is Voegelin who used the phrase "Leap of Being" to characterize the fifth century B.C. in describing the transformation from a cosmological to a philosophical world-view based on consciousness. His contention is that a unique transformation of human nature took place as the order of the myth gave way to the order of the soul under the influence of philosophy, which was in its unique form a product of that change. On the subject of Fragment 54 Voegelin finds an exalted but rational language to explain his insight. As we pick up the argument, Voegelin is speaking about the philosophical search for the new order of the human soul:

> The new deliberateness and radicalism of the inquiry can perhaps be sensed most clearly in the famous fragment: "character — to man — demon." It is not easy to gauge the full importance of the fragment because it is isolated. In a first approach one might attribute to it as little technical meaning as possible and consider it no more than a formulation in opposi-

tion to conventional opinions about character as the inner and demon as the external factor of human fate. Even if we exert such caution, there still remains the important fact that the demon is immanentized and identified with character (*ethos*). If, however, we put the fragment into the context of Pythagorean conception of the soul (a procedure that seems well justified), then it identifies the *daimon* in the Pythagorean sense with that structure of the soul which Heraclitus designates by the term *ethos*. This identification would imply the momentous break with the archaic inseparable connection of immortality with divinity. The soul, in order to be immortal, would not have to be a *daimon*; we would advance from a theomorphic conception of the soul to a truly human one. The basis for a critical, philosophical anthropology would be created.[31]

The key to Voegelin's analysis is the identity, or unity, established in the fragment between *ethos* and *daimon*, as opposed to a traditional religious formulation that frames a duality of human nature in which we possess mortal and immortal aspects, a mortal body and an immortal soul, and thus exist in the dualistic tension of a split nature. What Voegelin suggests to me, and I cannot attribute the following wording to him, is that the fragment could imply that human nature as a whole is in essence a spiritual nature or that human beings possess a unique spiritual ethos. As we stated earlier, Being in Becoming and Becoming in Being.

When Voegelin establishes the identity of *ethos* with *daimon*, we are presented with a two-headed coin, one side being *ethos* and the other, *daimon*. In Sanskrit, the term *sam-*

---

31. Eric Voegelin, *The World of the Polis*. Louisiana State University Press, Baton Rouge, 1957, p. 224.

sara, or "cycle of life" embodies the Eastern concept of the great wheel of existence in which individuals work out their *karma,* the Sanskrit term from the root *kri* meaning "action." In Hinduism each person must work out the burden of past action before returning to the Absolute as a purified soul. The cycle of *samsara* continues until all karmic debt is paid.

The Greek concept of karma reflects a similar cyclical destiny. The great myths upon which Homeric legend and Greek tragic drama are founded depend heavily upon the working out of family guilt and the suffering caused by sins passed from fathers to sons and mothers to daughters. The term *daimon* is often used to characterize such debt and suffering. The houses of Atreus and Thebes both catalogue the passing on of the curses of past sin to so-called innocent children. Part of the pathos of the Oedipus cycle is the supposed innocence of Oedipus as he struggles to work out his inherited karmic debt. For Oedipus, it is clear that his *ethos* is the same as his *daimon,* if we accept that what happens to him in killing his father and marrying his mother is the direct result of karmic debt or, in a manner of speaking, is simply the result of who he is. What is often forgotten in the story, however, is that the act of blinding himself is a specific choice made in the moment, and the transcendence of his suffering in the much later *Oedipus at Colonus* is characteristic of a man freed from his demonic past by virtue of character. In other words, we have to see and understand the whole story before the relation of *ethos* and *daimon* are understood.

Living in the cultural crossroads of Ephesus, Heraclitus would certainly have been aware of both the Hellenic view of demonic powers and its similarity to Eastern karmic philosophy. The similarity must be reflected in the term *daimon* as used in his famous aphorism. Character in a human being is initially defined by the karmic debt brought into the world at birth. However, far from being fated to suffer from that debt, the individual must be capable, through conscious insight and knowledge of the Logos, to overcome and transcend that so-called destiny. Knowledge will make us free. The aim is to become free of *samsara*.

To return for a moment to Voegelin's conclusions, we do indeed need in our own postmodern culture "a critical, philosophical anthropology." Some progress in this direction is evident in the important contribution being made by the various schools of consciousness, and in the published works of Mircea Eliade, Joseph Campbell, Gregory Bateson and the timely re-publication of the works of Ananda Coomaraswamy, who almost single-handedly brought an enlightened Eastern tradition to the attention of the West.[32] In addition, new thinking from the inspirations of Carl Jung as advanced by James Hillman, Robert Sardello, Thomas Moore and others in the archetypal psychology movement is shaping the dynamics of the order of the soul within a spectrum of human nature previously reduced by scientific materialism. Finally, the works by Sri Aurobindo introduce what is called an Integral Yoga which anticipates a full fusion of Eastern and Western influences leading toward a world transformation. These current trends echo the Great Leap of Being in which Heraclitus participated twenty-five hundred years ago. Or so it appears at present.

Rather than presenting a theomorphic vision of the soul, that is, one which has its basis in divine form or having its derivation in divine revelation (as articulated by Christian theology, for example), Heraclitus suggests that although human disposition is essentially different from the divine, nonetheless it has its own unique spiritual ethos by virtue of the lawful workings of the Logos. Such may be the intended meaning of Fragment 12: **Human nature does not have true judgment, but divine nature does.** Voegelin suggests that this

---

32. *Metaphysics and Traditional Art and Symbolism,* ed. Roger Lipsey. Bollingen Series, Princeton University Press, Princeton.

fragment, in which we translate *ethos* loosely as "human nature" suggests that *ethos* must have a range of meanings beyond character; it must designate the nature of a being in general, whether human or divine."[33] It should be clear, however, that nature in this context is not the Greek *physis*. Such arguments lead us to conclude that *ethos* in Heraclitus cannot simply mean "character" as we normally accept the term.

Finally, Fragment 54 may also frame another, less overtly spiritual meaning, but one central to the overall aim of Heraclitus. If we think of the word *destiny* as expressing limitation or even ground of being, then *ethos anthropoi daimon* may imply that a true human nature itself is our destiny. In other words, once we know who we are (**I searched my nature**), our destiny is to pursue that knowledge. We are what we seek to know about ourselves. The question then becomes to what extent human beings have the potential to change or transform their nature so as to manifest that knowledge as character. If we are asleep most of the time, then sleep is our nature. Here we are, twenty-five hundred years afterward, still exploring the possibilities of human nature suggested by Heraclitus and not necessarily getting any closer to an answer. In this case, Fragment 54 might imply something like "An evolved human nature is our destiny." Such a fanciful translation, however, strays too far from *ethos anthropoi daimon*. It is a fanciful projection of the sentence rather than a translation.

Our task, then, if we would know the meaning of this key fragment, is to explore the other fragments for *ethos*, with the intent to relate its meaning to the Logos to see what, if any, genuine connection exists between human character and the universal power which "directs all things."

---

33. *World of the Polis*, p. 224.

Our first stop is to look again at Fragment 12: **Human nature does not have true judgment, but divine nature does.** As mentioned above, "human nature" here is a translation of *ethos* and intends a sense of the human constitution, how we are made up by nature. It is clearly not "character." Kirk and Raven also translate *gnomas* as "true judgment" whereas Jones prefers "understanding,"[34] which seems to imply a lower level of mental apprehension than is intended in the fragment. If divine *gnosis* or "knowing" is the same as true judgment, then Heraclitus establishes a hierarchy of judgment and wisdom in the cosmos by affirming the limitations of human understanding in relation to divine knowledge. In this limited human condition we must proceed by signs and must be prepared for surprises from the hidden realm of the divine *ethos*. In other words, narrowly *human* perception has no insight; only *divine* wisdom does. Heraclitus tells us that if we would partake in the Logos, we must acquire the force of divine insight.

Fragment 5 reminds us of this limitation in the sensory realm: **Eyes and ears are bad witnesses, especially if we have souls that do not understand their language.** And yet, this fragment provides a window on divine insight by giving the human being *with a properly aligned soul* the potential to properly understand the play of the senses in the cosmos. If the soul is properly attuned, sensory experience, or the experience of everyday life, may be a means by which higher knowledge is acquired. Heraclitus speaks directly of his own experience in Fragment 4: **I [personally] prefer the things which yield to seeing, hearing and thus to perception.** We are able to avoid contradiction in these two fragments by making the distinction between most human beings and the understanding of the philosopher whose soul is attuned, that is, in harmony with the Logos. Also, if we remember that

---

34. *Hippocrates*, p. 501.

Heraclitus searched his own nature, he emphasizes that he did so by interacting with the world and not by sitting in the dark, lost in thought.

Proper perception of the language of the senses means that the intellect or reasoning faculty apprehends the laws behind the sensory impressions and is therefore seeing or hearing with divine understanding. This fragment raises the specter of "illusion," which is a sensory impression without insight. Both the Eastern and Western transcendental sources (as characterized by Idealism) make this distinction clear. In American idealism, Ralph Waldo Emerson's vision picks up this theme. "We should say with Heraclitus: 'Come into this smoky cabin; God is here also: approve yourself to him.'"[35] Emerson's smoky cabin (his translation) is the place of illusions in which visitors cannot see beyond the smoke. Emerson articulates the theme in his essay on illusions:

> Every god is there sitting in his sphere. The young mortal enters the hall of the firmament; there is he alone with them alone, they pouring on him benedictions and gifts, and beckoning him up to their thrones. On the instant, and incessantly, fall snowstorms of illusions. He fancies himself in a vast crowd which sways this way and that, and whose movement and doings he must obey: he fancies himself poor, orphaned, insignificant. The mad crowd drives hither and thither, now furiously commanding this thing to be done, now that. What is he that he should resist their will, and think or act for himself? Every moment new changes and new showers of deceptions to baffle and distract him. And when, by and by, for an instant, the air clears and the cloud lifts a little, there

---

35. R. W. Emerson, *Works*, Harvard University Press, Cambridge, 1901, vol. x, p. 97.

are the gods still sitting around him on their thrones,
— they alone and him alone.[36]

Ordinary human experience is characterized by constant distracting movement, and yet our youth (the impressionable soul) does have a natural place in the divine firmament if only it will remain still for a moment. However, the youth can hardly see through the moist clouds. He cowers in the door, afraid to enter. This philosophical sleep is the condition in which the "many" flounder and misread the language of the senses. Plutarch reports Heraclitus as saying, " . . . there is one world in common for those who are awake, but that when men are asleep each turns away to a world of his own."[37] This reference may be Plutarch's sense of Fragment 2: **It is necessary, therefore, to obey the universal; but although the Logos is universal, most people live as though they had a private understanding,** or it may be a separate and related fragment. In either case, the relationship to philosophical sleep and to living in a world of our own is clear enough.

When we say that people live in a world of their own, we usually mean that they have a limited view of reality or that they are out of touch with the "real" world. Heraclitus is not speaking here of not paying attention to the world's events or even of ignoring the needs of the community. Even less is he speaking of being wrapped up in our own egos, concerned only with our own interests. The theme is metaphysical, about being aware of the broad truth of things, of knowing what directs all things through all things. There are, then, two kinds of people in the world: those (most people) who live with a private (closed) understanding and those who are able to live in the open in the presence of the Logos.

---

36. R. W. Emerson, *Essays and Lectures,* Library of America, New York, 1983, p. 1123.
37. Jones, XCII, p. 499.

Moist and Dry Souls

Fragments 36, 37, and 38 refer to the human soul as either moist or dry. Another reference comes from Aristotle, who in his *De Anima* (I. 405 a, 25-28) says, crediting but not quoting Heraclitus, "Soul is the vaporization out of which everything else is derived."[38] We do not know to what extent this idea belongs to Heraclitus or whether Aristotle is drawing this conclusion from the references we already possess, but the concept of vaporization related to soul helps us with the following fragments.

Fragment 36 reads, **It is death for souls to become water, as it is death for water to become earth; water comes to be from earth, as soul comes from water.** If we read "death" here as destruction or loss of material nature, we can see a range of alteration in the transformation of water into earth and earth into water and then water into soul. Soul has a nature of its own, we would assume, not necessarily connected directly with human nature but obviously influenced by it. The key is a range of refinement into aspects of animation. Another writer, Arius Didymus, has Heraclitus saying, **"Souls are vaporized from what is moist."**[39] This phrasing suggests that when human beings are born, their souls are formed in water, or, as Wheelwright phrases it, "vaporized from that generative moisture," which he objectifies as the womb.[40] From that state the soul dries or vaporizes into divine nature through the influence of higher consciousness.

Given the general range of this argument, however, Heraclitus is probably not being too literal here, even in his choice of very literal terms like moist and dry. And then again, per-

---

38. Wheelwright, p. 144.
39. Ibid.
40. Ibid, p. 63.

haps Heraclitus was more of an alchemist than we know. What may be the Platonic case is that the human soul descends into life in the moisture of human birth and ascends through consciousness to a dry or ethereal state by a process somewhat akin to vaporization. The image suggests a gradual refinement to the ether, to use the ancient term, if a human being does not prevent this crucial transformation from occurring through ignorance, drunkenness, neglect and sleep. Other terms we might employ are corporeal form transformed into incorporeal form, an image that negates the medieval debate about which state the soul possesses.

Fragment 38 says, **When he is drunk, thus having his soul moist, a man is led about by an immature boy, stumbling and not knowing where he is going.** In our sleeping, drunken state, the soul has little chance of transformation. Another spurious fragment has Heraclitus saying, "Souls take pleasure in becoming moist,"[41] suggesting that Freud's death-seeking pleasure principle seduces us into destructive behavior, literally at the cost of our souls. From Fragment 38 we also understand that the moist soul is immature; it knows nothing and has little or no sense of direction.

Fragment 37 states the matter directly. **A dry soul is wisest and best.** Wisdom is the quality human beings seek to acquire in order to apprehend the Logos and to live a focused life. A dry soul, having been vaporized from its initial condition by the fire of the passion to know or the natural sense of loss that comes from suffering, leads us in that wise direction.[42] The image is, in fact, a telling one. We

---

41. Ibid, p. 58.
42. It is not the place here to pursue the theme of suffering as it stimulates philosophic inquiry, but during the period of the "Leap of Being" the teachings of the Buddha, in particular, had their basis in the inquiry into the nature of human suffering. Also, Ortega y Gasset in his *Loss of Self in Art* suggests that the philosophic impulse arises from "feeling shipwrecked upon things."

do not picture a besotted individual to be in possession of wisdom.

Part of the mythology of Greek antiquity combines all of these images into one telling image. The goddess Demeter, part of the wisdom tradition as Earth Mother and Divine Nature, takes up the role of the nurse of mankind while she searches for her daughter Persephone (a symbol of the lost soul). As part of her nursing duties to the young Prince Demophoon of Eleusis, she has the frightening habit of placing him in the hot coals of the fire each night in order to make him immortal. One night, his moist-souled mother sees this activity and reacts in horror, whereupon Demeter reveals herself in all her glory and denounces human beings as ignorant. The image of the young soul being "vaporized" corresponds to the wisdom of the dry soul. When myths lose their meaning and understanding gives way to fairy tale, language must necessarily change accordingly, and philosophy takes up the cause of meaning.

A connection to this imagery and to fire (that which vaporizes) emerges in Fragment 30:

What we call "hot" seems to be immortal and to apprehend all things: to see and hear and know all things, both present and future. This otherness, then, the diversity of the all, when things become clouded, went out to the furthermost revolution, and seems to me to have been what was called ether by the men of old.

Images in this fragment suggest the personified Sun, Zeus as Bright Consciousness, and the countless stars out in space, all suggesting the realms of heaven found in medieval cosmology. All this imagery points to a direction for human *ethos*: an evolution toward the dry and thus hot incorporeal state most associated with divinity. This break with the archaic culture of Homer and Hesiod, where gods and heroes lived in and breathed the corporeal air, epitomizes in Heraclitus the crucial break with the past.

A dry soul, therefore, was one capable of making that crucial break with the past and going on to new transcendental territory, a place where the Logos has its being and toward which human *ethos* must tend. Heraclitus employs imagery of transcendence here to emphasize the direction of our proper attentions. One of the aphorisms of the Pythagorean school was that human beings possessed sight in order to study astronomy and hearing in order to study harmony.

Human beings contain in their psychic nature the four elements. Fire, the core element of change and transformation, works its evaporative magic in our being when we turn the fire in the mind to clarity rather than confusion as represented by the seeming chaos of the world order. As the transforming element, fire is capable of affecting fundamental change in our perceptions. The fire of mind, with its burning faculties of reason, intellect, imagination and memory, links us to the Logos, which in turn is made manifest to us by the *daimon* within. This dry fire of the mind has the transformative power to evaporate the moist conditions of human existence, which are embodied in our private, separate, pleasure-seeking worlds. If, as Heraclitus says, "all things are One," it is clarity of mind purified by fire that allows us to perceive, experience, and partake in that unity.

As an instigator, that is, one who used language to create as well as to describe, Heraclitus prods the sleeping to awaken to the true direction of human *ethos*. We all begin in this moist, sleeping state. Several fragments run together state the case well enough. First, Fragment 6: **When they are spoken to, the ignorant are like the deaf: they bear witness to the proverb that when present they are absent.** Join this to a dubious fragment from the Loeb collection:

Many do not interpret aright such things as they encounter, nor do they have knowledge of them when they have learned, though they seem to themselves so to do . . . knowing neither how to listen nor how to speak.[43]

These thoughts describe the difficulty of waking up philosophically and the doubly dangerous state of assuming a knowledge we do not in fact possess.

Help, however, sometimes comes from outside. A dubious fragment attributed to Heraclitus may in fact come from Aristotle and suggests that "Every creature is driven to pasture with blows."[44] Our desire is to remain asleep, to stay in the comfort zone of the barn, to be fed, to be safe, to be content.[45] The pasture is where the work is done (our professional "fields"), and we do not go to the pasture willingly. In the pasture we are exposed, vulnerable to the elements and to accident and disappointment. It is where we are tested and where we prove our worth.

Nature provides us with more images of life's range of experience. We work in our fields. The woods provide mystery and escape. Water is the abyss, the element of dreams and death. The mountain offers transcendence and aspiration, the deserts solitude and testing. Civilized life, especially in cities, effectively masks all these distinctions. In cities, so devoid of natural settings, our experience is flattened into a seamless daily existence. To be conscious, we must be shaken loose from our routines and see our "fields" as the pasture of

---

43. Jones, III, V, VI, p. 473.
44. Jones, LV, p. 489.
45. See Plato's allegory of the cave in the *Republic*, Book VII. The analogy is very similar in picturing human beings content in their shadowed world until one is moved to break free and climb to the light.

our awakening rather than merely the expression of our ambitions or the source of our daily bread.

The "work" we do in the culture, Heraclitus would have us see, is not the work we are meant to do. Rather, we reduce ourselves to habitual patterns of activity and never take advantage of nature's transitions, to go from field to woods or from lake to mountain or desert. To pass from the field into the woods, for example, is to enter a special realm, a private place where we can seize the opportunity for conscious reflection. Emerson said in *Nature,*

> In the woods too, a man casts off his years, as the snake his slough, and at what period soever of life, is always a child. In the woods, is perpetual youth. Within these plantations of God, a decorum and sanctity reign, a perennial festival is dressed, and the guest sees not how he should tire of them in a thousand years. In the woods, we return to reason and faith. There I feel that nothing can befall me in life, — no disgrace, no calamity, (leaving me my eyes,) which nature cannot repair.[46]

These observations already reflect a conscious awareness of the movement away from the common condition in one fully conscious individual. For the many, however, the need for awakening may mean receiving a decisive blow. There is the old story about the man passing by the farm and seeing the farmer beating his mule in the head with a piece of lumber. When asked why he is beating the animal so, the farmer replies, "I ain't beatin him. I'm just gittin' his attention." It is an instigation at the most primitive level. Heraclitus knew

---

46. R.W. Emerson, *Nature,* p. 10.

that we must be beaten into the self-reflective pasture to begin the task of waking to consciousness.

Many students give themselves willingly into the hands of a spiritual teacher, for example, because they have become convinced through habitual failure they will sleep otherwise. There seem to be few with the discipline to proceed alone, without outside help. In some traditions, such as Zen Buddhism, the teacher provides actual blows with a bamboo switch to keep the student awake during the practice of meditation. It is even suggested that a well-timed blow will induce instant enlightenment.

Heraclitus used his aphorisms as such blows. Since he was dealing with the mind, he used mind-blows to awaken his students. Fragment 20, **Good and bad are the same,** is such a blow. If we lapse, as indeed we often do, into the easy duality of good things and bad things, into the world where we soothe our own choices by society's arbitrary divisions, we need such a blow to bring our attention to the Logos, where the truth resides. Good and bad are nothing but culturally induced opinions, the *doxa* where Plato told us there resides nothing but death. Health is good, disease bad, and yet without disease we would have no awareness of health, of the illusion of being "disease free."

Another such psychic blow is Fragment 32: **The sun is new each day.** Naive or scientifically arrogant commentators like Aristotle have said that this fragment illustrates the ignorance of earlier thinkers, who imagined that the gods created the sun each day and drove it into the sky by chariot. On the contrary, Heraclitus is striking a blow at our habitual thinking that sees one day as like every other, a dulling repetition of similar dawns. Consciousness demands awareness that each moment is a window through which the wakened state perceives the secrets of the Logos. In this world, the sun *is* new each moment. Its fires burn ever new and we are reminded of the waters of the stream into which we can never step twice.

In Fragment 40 we see the effects of this psychic sleep: **At night man kindles a light for himself when his eyes fail to see; thus in life, he is in contact with the dead when asleep and with the sleeper when awake.** The hierarchy of wakened states is clearly established here so that those deluded into thinking they are philosophically awake will have no doubt as to their true state. The moist soul sleeps in a drunken stupor, drugged as it were by things and by the wrongful perception that what our eyes and ears report, without a dry soul to mediate, tells the true story of experience. We become captured and lulled by flickering images.

In effect, we kill our opportunities through superstition and are like murderers who wash bloody hands with blood to cleanse our consciences. Fragment 48 explains: **They purify themselves in vain of blood-guilt by defiling themselves with blood, as though one who had stepped into mud were to wash with mud; he would appear insane if anyone noticed him doing this. Further, they pray to statues as if one were to carry on a conversation with houses, not recognizing the true nature of gods and spirits.**

According to Demosthenes, the initiates of the Orphic Mysteries were purified by immersing themselves in mud, not, to be sure, to cleanse themselves of mud by washing in mud, but the implication still holds. The symbolism no doubt included a subsequent ritual bathing, thus sloughing off the layers of earthly identification in order to become transformed into a more ethereal state. But Heraclitus here wishes to exorcize his culture from the baser sacrifices of the arcane practices of the day.

We are able to see in this fragment a general comment about fruitless behaviors in the name of blind religious faith. In these instances Heraclitus placed himself directly in opposition to the religious excesses of his native Ephesus. Presumably, he was forced to do so in order to rain more verbal blows upon the ignorance of the Many. What he saw was a complete separation between the pleading supplicant and the opaque god, each, humans and gods, in a world of their own.

The fragments we possess exhibit two main characteristics: harsh criticism and intentional obscurity, or blows and riddles. These two characteristics reflect the needs of human *ethos*. On the one hand we slip into banal, habitual behaviors and need blows to be shaken from them. On the other, we require hints of a new level of perception and must penetrate the mind-bending riddle to find it. This challenge, for which Heraclitus was justly famous as The Dark One, came not so much from the desire to hide his true meaning from the philistines who might stumble upon his writings and mock his efforts, but rather from the necessity in which the true nature of things had to be presented.

Language is a self-reflective instrument. When we speak our thoughts, the thoughts return to our ears as formed understanding, heard by our own minds and judged true or not in the crucible of our powers of discrimination. Without language, in other words, ultimate meaning *(telos)* cannot be found. Without such meaning, we are absent in existence, having no presence. We simply pass through, like Mayflies, in a day. Thus, when language presents us with both blows and riddles, we are stretched and have a chance to extend existence from Being into a Becoming.

In Fragment 41 we have an example of language as a foundation of being:

[According to Heraclitus] we acquire understanding by drawing in the Logos through breathing, as we are forgetful when asleep, we regain our senses when we

wake up again. For in sleep, when the channels of perception are shut, our mind is shaken loose from its surroundings, and breathing is the only point of contact to hold on, rather like a root; being separated then, our mind loses its former power of memory. But in the waking state it again looks out through the channels of perception as through a kind of window, and meeting with the surroundings it puts on the power of Reason.

The power of Reason, that attribute of the mind capable of gathering to itself the data necessary for self-knowledge and psychic illumination, "looks out through the channels of perception" to a new dawn. This fragment comes to us through Sextus Empiricus, the Greek physician and skeptic, and may have a note of his well-documented attitudes, but many scholars, including Kirk and Raven, credit Heraclitus in full for it. The fragment does not "sound" like Heraclitus (neither blow nor riddle), but it expresses nonetheless an important Heraclitean principle: sense-based perception leading out to the transcendent "power of Reason."

Kant described Reason as "the lawgiver to Nature," suggesting the connection (also made through the Greek of *logos* and *logismos*) to the highest faculty of mind. In another context, related by their philosophical sympathies, Thomas Carlyle described the work of Novalis in exactly the same vein.

The aim of Novalis' whole philosophy, we might say, is to preach and establish the majesty of Reason, in that stricter sense; to conquer for it all the provinces of human thought, and everywhere reduce its vassal Understanding into fealty, the right and only useful relation for it. Mighty tasks of this sort lay before him of which, in these writings of his, we trace only scattered indications. In fact, all that he has left is in the shape of Fragment detached expositions and combinations, deep, brief glimpses: but such seems to be their general tendency. [47]

So close is this insight to the work of Heraclitus that Carlyle might as well have been speaking of his work and thought. It also suggests that should we wish to expand our understanding of Heraclitus, we could not do better than to have the fragments of Novalis at our side.

What the world presents to our Reason is filtered through the realms of undifferentiated consciousness, which initially is as formless as the void. When Heraclitus suggests that we become intelligent by breathing in the Logos, he describes in physical terms the process by which consciousness forms itself into coherence, into thought, and eventually into language. To come closest to the Logos, this process in human beings must come closest to fire, which is the nature of the Logos. As Kirk and Raven explain it,

> The soul in its true and effective state is made of fire
> . . . . The implication is not only that the soul is fiery,
> but also that it plays some part in natural change. It
> comes into being from moisture . . . and is destroyed
> when it turns entirely into water. The efficient soul is
> dry, that is, fiery.[48]

---

47. Lee Rust Brown, *The Emerson Museum*, Harvard University Press, Cambridge, 1997, p. 104.
48. Kirk and Raven, p. 206. In the Vedic tradition, the soul after death returns according to its state either to the sun (if dry) or to the moon (if moist). Those souls drawn to the watery moon are destined to return to an earthly existence, until they eventually return to the sun, their natural "home."

That the Logos is also "word" makes the connection between the power and principle that "directs all things" and the way in which language serves as the instrument of the Logos in human nature (*ethos*). It is clear then that one of the great accomplishments of Heraclitean thought resides in the firm connection he makes between the Logos as divine instigator and language as human power. As he says in Fragment 57,

Those who speak with sense rely on what is universal, as a city must rely on its law, and with much greater reliance. For all human laws are nourished by one divine law; for it has as much power as it wishes and is sufficient for all with more left over.

In this fragment human laws refer to those laws (*nomoi*) derived from the Logos, which in turn reflect wisdom in the expressive human soul. Added to this thought and connected naturally to it, is the assurance that the Logos has unlimited power. If we in our ignorance wonder at the dearth of creative consciousness, which seems to be the lot of human life, the fault lies, dear Brutus, not in the stars but in ourselves. We just have to get out of the barn into the field where the power is emanating like bright sunshine.

Fragment 39 defines further the unlimited power of the human soul once realized. **You would not find out the limits of the soul, even by traveling along every path: so deep a logos does it have.** Here, *logos* in the fragment has the sense of extent or measure. Once again we are shown how the Logos penetrates every sphere or layer of the cosmos. Once we see clearly that with a dry (fiery) soul we are able to participate in both the wisdom and the power of the Logos, we are given through negation (*apophasis*) an unlimited view of the boundless nature of the soul. We are told not to travel an earthly path in our seeking. Instead comes the assurance that what we seek, the *telos* or goal of human existence, has no limits. What we experience may have limits, but the soul which forms human *ethos* has none. The Logos exists in the *apeiron*.

In the spirit of Heraclitus we conclude this section of our inquiry with the clear ambiguity that human *ethos* is a reflection of the order of the soul, which has limitless boundaries and participates and yet does not participate in the realm of divinity, giving us uncertain assurances of our immortal mortality. Or, as the master has it in Fragment 46, **Immortal mortals, mortal immortals, living their death and dying their life.** The riddle here unravels the nature of human *ethos* as both Being and Becoming. Aurobindo helps us immeasurably here. He says about this fragment, "The immanence of the immortal principle in man, the descent of the gods into the workings of mortality was almost the fundamental idea of the mystics."[49] As we shall see later on, the interface between the immortalizing human mind and the mortalizing descent of the divine into human life expresses itself in Plato's description of the role of *eros* in bridging the gap between the mortal and immortal worlds.

Finally, then, after an amplification of Fragment 54 that more than declares it to be the central idea in the mystical philosophy of Heraclitus, we arrive at an offer of translation, an approximation of *ethos anthropoi daimon* in the context of a broad view of the essence of human character/nature and in the context of gender-neutral preferences. We are indebted to Sri Aurobindo for his sense of *daimon* as "divine force."

Fragment 54 reads, then, **For human beings, character is the divine force.** Enough mystery remains to entice us to fur-

49. Aurobindo, p. 4.

ther approximations, but the central image remains. For human beings, immortal mortals, it is character that allows us to partake of Being and to reach into the divine realm and, perhaps, even into its nature.

The next step takes us up into the realm of *telos,* the goal or aim of human life in its transformative destiny. Having given birth to soul, we then develop it into an immortal *daimon.*

TELOS

All of the fragments taken together give a sense of direction and purpose (*telos*), a glimpse of a resolution to the tension of Being and Becoming. This teleological frame in Heraclitus takes us to a different, a higher platform, if not an ultimate one. The fragments dealing with limited human *ethos* do not merely shatter our illusions of competence and then leave us hanging. Nor does Heraclitus leave us with the comfortless notion that this ever-changing flux we call reality is its own end, which is to say, no end at all but ceaseless change. There is for Heraclitus someone or something at the helm, which in turn implies a vessel with a rudder actually going some-where.

In 1964, the British novelist John Fowles published a series of personal notes under the title *The Aristos*. In it he credited the fragments of Heraclitus as being the impetus of his own musings, as well as of the aphoristic style of his own fragmentary notes. Fowles claimed that he was advised against publishing *The Aristos* by all who read the manu-script, presumably because of its didactic tone and fragmen-tary style. It seemed presumptuous. It seemed to those he consulted as if Fowles could not be bothered to frame a coherent argument. In fact, the book, although not widely read, was received with enthusiasm because of its honesty and depth of perception.

The purpose of *The Aristos* was to issue a warning, to offer a plea for an authentic individualism in the face of ram-pant conformism. Much of it had been written before John F. Kennedy's assassination, before the Berkeley riots, and before the Beatles. In his preface to the 1970 edition Fowles took the book in a slightly different direction. He refers to British philosopher Karl Popper's book *The Open Society* in which Heraclitus is referred to as the grandfather of totalitarianism. According to Popper, the elitism inherent in the fragments gave strength to those (the self-styled *aristoi)* who would seize control of political power and dictate to the Many *(hoi polloi).* Popper saw in Hitler the grim results of this elitism. Fowles responded to this criticism in his preface:

> Now Heraclitus saw mankind divided into a moral and intellectual elite (the *aristoi,* the good ones, not — this is a later sense — the ones of noble birth) and an unthinking, conforming mass — *hoi polloi,* the many. Anyone can see how such a distinction plays into the hands of all those subsequent thinkers who have advanced theories of the master-race, the super-man, government by the few or by the one, and the rest. One cannot deny that Heraclitus has, like some in itself innocent weapon left lying on the ground, been used by reactionaries: but it seems to me that his basic contention is *biologically* irrefutable.[50]

Saying that the fragments resemble a weapon left lying around for anyone to use misstates both their impact and their intent, or teleological purpose. The fragments are more like scalpels, capable of being used by a skilled surgeon to excise a tumor, but not in themselves intended to maim. Can a madman kill with a scalpel? Assuredly so. Does that fact recommend foregoing the use of scalpels altogether? Obviously not. Similarly, Emerson's *Self-Reliance* was used by Social Darwinians to justify economic survival of the fittest. Does that misapprehension negate the philosophical truth of *Self-Reliance?*

That Fowles sees the division of human beings into the Few and the Many as biologically irrefutable strikes closer to home, but even here the term "biological" has about it too

---

50. Fowles, *The Aristos,* New American Library, New York, 1970, p. 9.

much the ring of genetic determinism. The question becomes then: upon what basis does Heraclitus make this division into *aristoi* and *hoi polloi*? Surely it is not a matter of intelligence or some sense of "native ability."

The answer must arise from his *telos*, his vision of why he wrote what he wrote. And in this sense, it becomes even clearer that the fragments reflect a division based on consciousness, elitist though it might appear to be. Those prepared to delve into the mysteries of the Logos are those invited to enter the hut and gather around the stove where the gods dwell. As to the Many, Fragment 50 states the case well enough: **Those who sleep also share in the work of the cosmos.** "Everyone plays a role" is different from "everyone is given a role to play."

In terms of the *telos* of the work undertaken by either the Few or the Many, much depends upon one's sense of what Fowles calls "The Situation." He chose a metaphor to describe his vision of the modern situation, but it could also describe "the situation" of an ancient culture being separated from its myths.

> Humanity on its raft. The raft on the endless ocean. From his present dissatisfaction man reasons that there was some catastrophic wreck in the past, before which he was happy, some golden age, some Garden of Eden. He also reasons that somewhere ahead lies a promised land, a land without conflict. Meanwhile, he is miserably *en passage;* this myth lies deeper than religious faith.[51]

There are two significant features of this metaphor of the modern condition: the absence of a helmsman as the vessel becomes a rudderless raft drifting with the currents, and the

---

51. Ibid, 15.

dependence upon an ideal past out of which human beings have somehow fallen. In this climate or situation, the only *telos* possible is an existential one, stated by Fowles on the final page of his book:

> To accept one's limited freedom, to accept one's isolation, to accept this responsibility, to learn one's particular powers, and then with them to humanize the whole: that is the best [the *aristos*] for this situation.[52]

In the final analysis Fowles is not, then, a student of Heraclitus, but rather an existentialist who defines the Logos in his own terms as hazard.

What we may now see is that neither Popper's or Fowles' view of Heraclitus is accurate, at least in terms of the *telos* of his work. But, when we ask the Heraclitean fragments to reveal to us an end, a *telos* for which we might, as seeking human beings, give our attention and devotion, we do not receive an overt answer, although the fragments suggest that *telos* is a "directed" end. Not surprisingly, Heraclitus refrains from telling us, as the Stoics or the early Christian fathers did, something like, "Know the Logos as the will of God and follow it faithfully into the Kingdom." He similarly does not tell us to devote our lives to the *polis* in public service or to become the enlightened guardians of the people, although several fragments hint at the role played in the culture by those who are awake enough to be guardians.

It becomes necessary, therefore, in an effort to frame the fragments within the concept of *telos*, to move our inquiry to the greater context of the Leap of Being in order to shed light on this theme. In other words, what Heraclitus has to tell us

---

52. Ibid, 214.

can be found in his language in context, and that context is the great Leap of Being of 500 B.C.

To begin, we are helped by Fowles' observation that in our present situation we look back upon an ideal past, a golden age or Garden of Eden, out of which we have been driven by the vengeful God of Abraham for our sins. The great Leap of Being within which Heraclitus lived and wrote, changes this vision, moving away from such a past and instead framing an evolutionary vision based on leaps of consciousness. It may be argued that the teaching of Jesus, some five hundred years after Heraclitus, meant to build upon this Leap of Being, to teach that human beings, having been released from the bondage of the past into a new dispensation, can overcome the suffering of their various captivities. But Fowles is correct in saying that the myth of the golden age and the perfect Garden of Eden "lies deeper than religious faith." If we return to 500 B.C., we may see just how this new vision took shape in the traditions surrounding Ephesus and influencing Heraclitus.

A *telos* is more than a goal; it is also a place to stand, that place where Archimedes said he would need to stand if he were going to move the world. "Give me a place to stand," he said, "and I will move the Earth." Such a *logos*-statement comes from a fully formed *ethos*, one centered simultaneously in the world and in consciousness. As human beings we stand with one foot in the world order and the other in consciousness. Such a dual nature initiates the search for the true nature of *telos*, an end which harmonizes *physis* and *ethos* into unity.

A sense of that tension is expressed in Fragment 10: **Everything taken together is whole but also not whole, what is being brought together and taken apart, what is in tune and out of tune; out of diversity there comes unity, and out of unity diversity.** At the simplest level, the unity is the *telos* spoken of in most texts of the period.

What we learn from this tension is that we exist in at least one part of the mind in some state of "in-betweenness," what Plato called the *metaxy*. Two senses of this *metaxy* or "in-betweenness" find expression in the human condition. The first relates to the presence of suffering in human existence, resulting in detachment, and the second is the state of being best described by the Hindu Vedas as Nirvana, or bliss. From both these ideas came a proper sense of *telos* as the ground between the indeterminate Logos and the evolving *ethos* of the human being.

Voegelin's Leap of Being reached its apex when Heraclitus was in his prime, at the time when the great teachers of human suffering and transformation, Gautama the Buddha and Lao Tse (Master Lao) were probably active. In Ephesus, an important seat of the Earth Mother cult, the influence of Zoroastrianism would also have been felt, with its rituals of initiation into the mysteries of Mithras.[53] Modern scholarship is now convinced that the Book of Genesis was transcribed from the Hebrew oral tradition in the 6th century as well. From a slightly earlier period, the prophetic messages of Jeremiah (whose dates are usually set from 646 through the fall of Jerusalem in 587 B.C.) might well have been known and studied. Some interpreters suggest that Jeremiah's life and teaching created "a new covenant written in the heart"[54] which in turn paved the way for the image of the Suffering Servant of Deutero-Isaiah (also 6th century) and the new covenant of Christianity. The so-called Deutero-Isaiah stands even closer to the time of the Great Leap.

The effect of all these teachings was to establish an order of the soul and a new description of and approach to the

---

53. Mithras was a god of light who in primordial time slew a bull from whose blood sprang nature, including human life. Rituals of Mithraism involved slaughter of a bull and consecration with bread and wine, in the substance of which was the divine substance of eternal life.

54. *The Jerusalem Bible*, Doubleday and Co., New York, p. 1127

divine ground, one based on participation, rather than separation, and on the real potential of unity rather than a limiting duality. Seeking this potential union became the new *telos* of those who were initiates into its mysteries. In this totally new sense of being, Heraclitus wove his way through the Greek mythological corpus, the ancient Earth Mother cults, the sibylitic traditions of Delphi, the new Eastern mysticisms, and, quite possibly, the powerful new prophetic voices of Judaism to a wholly individual vision of human *ethos*.

The Prophet Jeremiah

We will now compare some of the Heraclitean fragments with texts from the same period in order to illustrate something of this more complete fabric of teaching. Following a basic chronology, we begin with Jeremiah, one of the major Hebrew prophets. The language we hear initially echoes language heard throughout the Torah, from Genesis on. Verses 9:22-24, for example, set the themes:

> Thus says Yahweh,
> "Let the sage boast no more of his wisdom,
> nor the valiant of his valor,
> nor the rich man of his riches!
>
> But if anyone wants to boast, let him boast of this:
> of understanding and knowing me.
> For I am Yahweh, I rule with kindness,
> justice and integrity on earth;
> yes, these are what please me
> — it is Yahweh who speaks."[55]

---

55. Jeremiah, 9:5, 22-24.

And Yahweh gives this message to his people through Jeremiah:

"Come back, disloyal children — it is Yahweh who speaks — for I alone am your Master. I will take one from a town, two from a clan, and bring you to Zion. I will give you shepherds after my own heart, and these shall feed you on knowledge and discretion. And when you have increased and become many in the land, then — it is Yahweh who speaks — no one will ever say again: Where is the ark of the covenant of Yahweh? There will be no thought of it, no memory of it, no regret for it, no making of another."[56]

The reference to the Ark of the Covenant may well relate to its presumed destruction when the temple fell in 587 B.C. The promised new covenant will be based on "knowledge and discretion" and will place greater responsibility on the people for their relationship to the divine ground in Yahweh, one based on "understanding and knowing me."

The tone of this message from Jeremiah marks a subtle change in the prophetic language of the Hebrews, and there is difference enough in hearing of a kind and just Yahweh to begin a new vision of the divine relation. And the possession of a written text available for study by pagan scholars shifts the ground of knowledge and inquiry to a new level. It is almost certain that the Torah and possibly the prophetic books as well were known to Heraclitus and others in Ephesus, so well known was it as a center of culture and so accessible was it to travelers from every point in the known world. When Heraclitus says in Fragment 13, **To God all things are beautiful, good and just, but human beings have supposed some things to be unjust, others just,** we hear a

---

56. Jeremiah, 3:14-17.

new sound which anticipates the Christian message five hundred years later.

Gautama The Buddha

In Buddhism, the problem of the existence of an eternal human *ethos* arises throughout the teaching of the Gautama. It is said that Buddhism was a reaction to abuses arising out of the Vedic tradition. If so, the main concern of the Buddhists was to correct a distortion in the Vedic view that an eternal human identity in the form of the personality was carried beyond the death of the body into the realm of Brahman. The issue was whether or not the *skandhas*, or elements of personality, were preserved after death as a coherent self. In one teaching, Gautama points out a worker in the woods gathering and burning grass and sticks. Sidney Spencer gives the following account:

> "Would you say that this man is gathering or burning us? You would not, and why?" "Because, lord, this is not our self nor of the nature of the self." So it is, the Buddha concludes, with the factors which make up men's individual being. "These are not yours; put them away." They have no more to do with the inmost Self of man (as the words may appear to imply) than the grass and sticks in the wood where he happens to be.[57]

While being careful to dismiss the eternal nature of certain elements of personality, the Buddha appears to preserve a greater Self in which human beings participate on a conscious level. This separation of ego identity from conscious

---

57. Spencer, p. 72. Text from *Majjhima Nikaya*, I: 140 ff.

participation in the divine ground is characteristic of the *telos*, or enlightenment of Buddhist doctrine, even without a deity.

The concept of Nirvana in Buddhism is an expression of that egoless state in which the saint participates without duality in the divine ground. If one is totally successful in this union, further incarnations are avoided and the self joins the greater Self in the eternal Reality. An example of how one approaches this *telos* are Gautama's last words to his disciples: "Live as those who have the Self as lamp, the Self as refuge, and no other." As Spencer reports,

> And again, it is urged that only in the light of this immanent principle can we understand such words as those of the *Dhammapada:* "Self is the lord of self: Self is the goal of self."[58]

Reference to the goal of self in the *Dhammapada* reminds us of the suffering associated with the struggle to abandon ego identity, to which we cling so tenaciously. In *Dhammapada* 342 we read:

> Men foregone by fear and longing wriggle this way and that like a hare ensnared;
> Held by the bonds of their attachments, again and again they undergo long miseries.[59]

In nearly all the references in Heraclitus to the Logos, we find similar language and a similar theme of letting go of the private view and embracing the universal one. Fragment 2 tells us, in effect, that to let go of the self in favor of the Self

---

58. Spencer, p. 73.
59. Ananda Coomeraswamy, *What is Civilization?* Lindisfarne Press, Hudson, N.Y., 1989, p. 105.

"... It is necessary, therefore, to obey the universal; but although the Logos is universal most people live as though they had a private understanding." To follow what is universal is the *telos* for which we struggle to awaken our higher understanding.

The Taoist Way

Tradition holds that Lao Tse (Master Lao) was born in 604 B.C.E. and that the text of the *Tao Te Ching* (Treatise of the Way and its Power) was written down as the great teacher was about to leave civilization for the last time to die in the mountains or to become a hermit there, or, perhaps, to transcend the physical plane altogether. Asked by the gatekeeper to write down his wisdom before he left, the master obediently took the time to describe the nature of the Tao and offer guidance to its realization. This tradition may reflect a desire to locate the beginnings of Taoism in history and may not reflect specific events.

Of particular interest to the general period of the Leap of Being is the tradition, particularly in China, of hermitism. It is as if the new transcendence had as one of its requirements a period of extended isolation, of radical withdrawal from civilized life. Certainly the stories attached to Heraclitus support that view. Only by totally withdrawing from normal life is the individual capable of achieving the desired awakened state. Such isolation is not for everyone. We have to be invited.

In its narrowest translation, the word Tao means Way, in the sense of *The* Way, just as *logos* means Word as the Christ in the Christian sense. And, too, in its broadest translation, *Tao* suggests the eternal law governing nature and the divine ground, just as does *logos* outside the Christian context. Indeed the similarities are so striking that Heraclitean thought lies much closer in meaning to Taoism than to Greek myth or examples of other Ionian philosophy.

Verse 77 of the *Tao Te Ching* addresses several aspects of the nature of the Tao and the role of the philosopher.

> The Tao of heaven is like the bending of a bow.
> The high is lowered, and the bow is raised.
> If the string is too long, it is shortened;
> If there is not enough, it is made longer.
>
> The Tao of heaven is to take from those who have too
> much and give to those who do not have enough.
> Man's way is different.
> He takes from those who do not have enough to give to
> those who already have too much.
> What man has more than enough and gives it to the
> world?
> Only the man of Tao.
>
> Therefore the sage works without recognition.
> He achieves what has to be done without dwelling on it.
> He does not try to show his knowledge.[60]

If we compare Verse 77 with Fragment 16 we note first the reference to the bow in relation to the Logos and the paradox of its tensions.

> They do not apprehend how being in conflict it still agrees with itself; there is an opposing coherence, as in the tensions of the bow and lyre.

In both instances we are presented with a metaphor of justice and its basis in the Tao and the Logos. The hierarchy, while establishing degrees of power and rule, nonetheless provides for all things according to justice and need. Nature

---

60. Lao Tsu, *Tao Te Ching,* translated by Gia-Fuller Feng. Vintage Books, New York, 1972.

operates in an opposed tension between the forces of insufficiency and excess, balancing accordingly. As was the case with Lao Tse and the Buddha, Heraclitus devoted himself to those who thirst for knowledge of the Logos and guided, not with an emphasis on learning, but a devotion to self-knowledge and understanding.

The Tao says, "He achieves what has to be done without dwelling on it." How is the philosopher to guide his disciple in the correct path? **Listen not to me but to the Logos.** Not by didacticism, that practice of drilling virtue into the habitual response mechanisms. The instigator, like the bow, pulls one way and the student flies in another. In the tension rests the power. This tension is expressed as well in Verse 81:

Truthful words are not beautiful.
Beautiful words are not truthful.
Good men do not argue.
Those who argue are not good.
Those who know are not learned.
The learned do not know.

The sage never tries to store things up.
The more he does for others, the more he has.
The more he gives to others, the greater his abundance.
The Tao of heaven is pointed but does no harm.
The Tao of the sage is work without effort.[61]

We will see clearly below in our discussion of Pythagoras and the temptations of learning and systems that an important distinction is being made here between knowing and learning, the separation between the vitality of intuitive knowledge and the dead matter of worldly knowledge. It is an image of human *ethos* we have seen already in Jeremiah.

---

61. Ibid.

The true philosopher/prophet ignores those already glutted on the world and its knowledge and serves instead the spiritually imprisoned seeking to be liberated. True wisdom, says the *Tao Te Ching* separates the wise from the ignorant:

> Heaven and earth are ruthless;
> They see the ten thousand things as dummies.
> The wise are ruthless;
> They see the people as dummies.[62]

Like Heraclitus, the emissaries of the Tao (the wise) see the Many as ignorant, hardly a very egalitarian point of view, but nonetheless spiritually accurate. In Fragment 12 Heraclitus makes a similar observation: **Human nature does not have true judgment, but divine nature does.** In this light, the point of view shifts. It is the wise, the ones who have acquired the gift of divine *ethos,* who are able to gauge human nature clearly. The "dummies" of the Tao are similarly those who are ignorant in the face of the Tao or who deny its presence altogether.

This theme in the teaching of Taoism may be more clearly illustrated in the work of Chuang Chou or Chuang Tse, the first known teacher of Taoism, who died in 286 B.C. Chuang's teaching describes that state of union with the Tao in which

> Being in a state of illumination he was able to gain the vision of the One. Being able to see the One, he was able to transcend the distinction of past and present; having transcended the distinction of past and present, he was able to enter the realm where life and death are no more.[63]

---

62. *Tao Te Ching,* verse 5.
63. Spencer, p. 99.

One feature of the Tao made explicit in the *Tao Te Ching* is its ultimately mysterious nature and quality, such that seekers as well as scholars are clearly discouraged from offering descriptive imagery. One imagines that Heraclitus, too, would have made the same disclaimer about the Logos if asked. To define is to confine, a risk we took earlier. Also, the closest we are able to approach the mystery of an evolved human *ethos* is the *metaxy*, that transformative in-between state in which we may participate but not dwell fully while we are breathing. The exceptions to this law are reserved for the enlightened few, the very few, such as the Buddha, who when asked to describe himself denied that he was a god or an angel or a wise man, but said merely, "I am awake."

Whether or not we are able to invite Heraclitus into this exalted company is beyond our scope. The cryptic Fragment 43, however, invites such speculation. It says, **In its presence [the Logos?], they rise up and become conscious guardians of the living and dead.** Since we cannot tell in what context this fragment might locate "presence," we are limited in how much we can say of its intent. The idea of conscious (or wakeful) guardians, however, does suggest that enlightened ones do rise up, bridging the *metaxy* in order to serve "the living and dead."

Other commentators have suggested that Heraclitus is referring here to angelic forms, immortals in the hierarchy who watch over the living and the dead. Such mythology in turn suggests that the fragment as a whole would then refer to a state in which the individual thus bridging the *metaxy* is greeted by those who have previously risen up and who serve there as guardians. To be in the *metaxy*, we imagine, is to be at the edge of the abyss in which total annihilation is all we can comprehend, unless, of course, we arrive as awakened souls supported by guardians of the light.

The Nature of the Metaxy

The *metaxy* is the new order of the Leap of Being. Although Heraclitus does not use the term among the fragments any more than he refers overtly to the *telos* of human transformation, these are the terms most expressive of the Logos of his teaching. Support for this view comes once again from the remarkable work of Eric Voegelin, whose analysis of the Leap of Being has directed scholarly attention to the 6th century B.C. as a watershed in human spiritual history.

Voegelin's analysis of the *metaxy* begins with Plato and the reference to it in the *Symposium* and the *Philebus*. In Voegelin's book *Anamnesis,* using a compact language designed to instigate as well as explicate, Voegelin describes the new order.

> Man experiences himself as tending beyond his human imperfection toward the perfection of the divine ground that moves him. The spiritual man, the *daimonion aner,* as he is moved in his quest of the ground, moves somewhere between knowledge and ignorance (*metaxy sophias kai amathias*). "The whole realm of the spiritual (*daimonion*) is halfway indeed between (*metaxy*) god and man" (*Symp*. 202a). Thus, the in-between — the *metaxy* — is not an empty space between the poles of the tension but the "realm of the spiritual"; it is the reality of "man's converse with the gods" (202-203), the mutual participation (*methexis, metalepsis*) of human in divine, and divine in human, reality. The *metaxy* symbolizes the experience of the noetic quest as a transition of the psyche from mortality to immortality.[64]

---

64. Eric Voegelin, *Anamnesis,* University of Missouri Press, Columbia and London, trans., ed. Gerhart Niemeyer, 1978, p. 103.

The first essential point of this description is that human *ethos*, or essential human nature, is moved by the imperfection in which it finds itself to the perfection of the divine ground which moves it. Our sense of imperfection comes not only from our own internal imperfections (seen as sin or disobedience in religious terms) but also from the perceived imperfections of the world in which we must live. A fundamental aversion to this imperfect world serves as an instigator to the seeking spirit and manifests itself in the artistic impulse as well as in social and political action.

The other essential point of Voegelin's description of the *metaxy* is that it is indeed "the realm of the spiritual." This distinction between the spiritual realm and the divine ground provides a space within which the conscious human being approaches and discovers a field of participation, or, in other words, a place to stand. This place to stand is expressed by Heraclitus in the realm of the *nous* or the intellect, where the *ethos* and the *Logos* find common ground.

The Nous

Among Greek philosophers the history of the use of the word *nous* begins with Heraclitus and reaches its zenith or nadir (depending on one's point of view) with Anaxagoras, the Athenian who lived during the Classical Period and was a friend and guide to Pericles. The key fragment from Anaxagoras, which Voegelin refers to as "the declaration of independence of the mind from the rest of being,"[65] reads as follows:

> The other things contain of all a part; the *Nous*, however, is something unlimited [*apeiron*] and self-ruling

---

65. Voegelin, *The World of the Polis*, p. 293.

[*autokrates*], and is mixed with no other thing, but is alone for itself.[66]

Voegelin's comment is crucial to an understanding of how the concept of mind as expressed by Heraclitus came to a bad end in classical Athens and how Parmenides' concept of Being was usurped by the new idea of a godlike human mind.

By making mind autonomous and not subject to limits, Anaxagoras may have created atheir being within the mind and have it exist eternally, but the result of his ingenious construct, as Voegelin explains, ". . . was purchased at the price of a serious destruction of the insights gained by Parmenides."[67] He is referring to Parmenides' careful exegesis of Being, which describes the dimensions of the human soul in its relation to the divine ground. In addition, we can also say that Anaxagoras took the concept of *nous* expressed by Heraclitus as the faculty within human *ethos* that as an evolved consciousness approached the *metaxy* and made it exclusively the point of contact with the divine ground.

Although the following is hardly a popular view, we can understand from this progression that the highly admired Classical Period of Greek history (from 480 to 338 B.C.) is really a period in which human beings became finally disconnected from their spiritual roots, their ground of being. In sculpture and architecture, in particular, the dominant theme is the glorification of the newly freed human being, a theme appropriated by the Italian Renaissance and characterized as humanism. The human being became the measure of all things. In contrast, the Archaic Period of the Leap of Being embodied the ideal projection of the human being as essentially spiritual in nature, grounded and yet released from the old mythological order by an enlightened consciousness.

---

66. Ibid.
67. Ibid.

For his part Heraclitus used *nous* in the fragments to illustrate the proper spiritual role of mind in human *ethos*. Before exploring that role, however, it will be useful to sketch in the view of the human mind in Greek philosophy in Plato and Aristotle and finally expressed in the work of Plotinus, the Neoplatonist of the second century A.D.

In Plato, the mind is that organ of perception that enables human beings to distinguish between the truth (*aletheia*) and opinion (*doxa*). The resulting knowledge, strengthened by innate wisdom, enables the seeker to perceive the true, transcendent Forms as opposed to the illusions of the world. The classic image of this distinction is illustrated in the allegory of the cave from the *Republic,* in which the cave-dwellers, who are chained to their places, face the shadows (symbols of the *doxa*) projected on the wall by ordinary human fire. Normal existence for these chained beings becomes an exercise in perfecting elaborate opinions about those shadows, and rewards (one imagines the Greek equivalent of a Ph.D.) are given to those who master the intricacies of shadow analysis.

Once an individual struggles free of the confining chains through the power of *eros*, or the passion to know the truth of things, it becomes possible to climb out of the cave into the blinding light of the truth, there to begin the journey of the newly awakened soul to the Good. Plato's vision is not presented as an event in history, but is a Genesis event within the mind and soul of the aspirant. It is a noetic (conscious experience from within) event and gives birth to the struggle of consciousness to realize its potential life in freedom and truth.

The logical or "scientific" extension of the creation of noetic consciousness begins in Aristotle's statement, "Human beings naturally desire to know." This desire eventually becomes differentiated into the components of mind with which we are the most familiar: intelligence, rational thinking, perception, and apprehension, all growing out of the *nous* but having different values. The natural philosophy of Aristotle, emerging as it does in a lower order of curiosity, had its extensions into logic, physics, and the beginnings of the biological and natural sciences, but stayed away from the function of mind initially developed by Heraclitus.[68]

It is not difficult to see just how the teleological vision of Heraclitus suffers reduction in the thinking of Aristotle. First, a relevant passage from *On the Parts of Animals,* Book I, Part 5:

> We therefore must not recoil with childish aversion from the examination of the humbler animals. Every realm of nature is marvelous: and as Heraclitus, when the strangers who came to visit him found him warming himself at the furnace in the kitchen and hesitated to go in, reported to have bidden them not to be afraid to enter, as even in that kitchen divinities were present, so we should venture on the study of every kind of animal without distaste; for each and all will reveal to us something natural and something beautiful. Absence of haphazard and conduciveness of everything to an end are to be found in Nature's works in the highest degree, and the resultant end of her generations and combinations is a form of the beautiful.

Here Aristotle's reduction of Heraclitus' experience at the stove to the curious examining of the humbler animals (undertaken without distaste) is typical of how the fragments were regarded as examples of past error and simplicity. In

---

68. Indeed, Aristotle's treatment of Heraclitus is patronizing. Much of the wisdom of the fragments is dismissed as wrong-headed and out-of-date in the light of the "new" scientific understanding described by Aristotle.

the *Physics*, Book III, Part 5b, for example, Aristotle takes issue with Fragment 24: **This cosmos [the unity of all that is] was not made by immortal or mortal beings, but always was, is and will be an eternal fire, arising and subsiding in measure.**

(b) Nor can fire or any other of the elements be infinite. For generally, and apart from the question of how any of them could be infinite, the All, even if it were limited, cannot either be or become one of them, as Heraclitus says that at some time all things become fire. (The same argument applies also to the one which the physicists suppose to exist alongside the elements: for everything changes from contrary to contrary, e.g. from hot to cold.)

This is a logical argument, sensible in its analysis and conclusions. If, however, Heraclitus is speaking about transformations of fundamental energy and the hidden nature of flux, fire becomes a metaphorical manifestation of such change, and as such a more esoteric, alchemical vision of transformation. Aristotle's *telos* is very different.

Six hundred years later, the revision of Platonic thought by Plotinus restored for a time the original Heraclitean mystic vision. In his more open concept of mind, Plotinus connected human *ethos* to the divine ground in specific and moving terms. His description is based on a hierarchy, a ladder of increasing complexity that works perfectly well in both directions but is really a top-down hierarchy, which we look at from the bottom up these days because our culture prefers bottom-up evolutionary thinking. The progression goes from inanimate matter at the very bottom to vegetative mind to sensation (as in the amoeba instinctively recoiling from light) to animal perception, to sensations of pleasure and pain, on to human image-making, to concepts and opinions, to the logical faculty, to creative reason to soul, to World soul (which exists at the psychic level), to *nous* (Plotinus' word for intuitive mind) to the Absolute or One, the Unity of all things.

This hierarchy includes in its movement a sense of the *metaxy* as interface and is part of the mysticism of Plotinus, whose core thinking is carried on into the Renaissance by Marcilio Ficino as a movement contrary to reductive humanism and then on into the so-called Perennial Philosophy of Gnosticism, and then into German Idealism and American Transcendentalism. Therefore, when we find voices like Emerson's referring back to Heraclitus, we are hearing the noetic strain of Plotinus carrying through despite the dominance in Western thought of Aristotelian philosophical movements, which includes Thomas Aquinas and most of modern scientific thought.

To return, now, to Heraclitus and his concept of the *nous,* we may be able to see how delicate a moment was this first attempt in the Leap of Being to form a frame of reference in language for the *nous*. In a controversial fragment referring to other philosophers, Heraclitus makes a distinction between learning (*didaskei,* from which we get our word didactic) and understanding (*noon*): "Much learning does not teach understanding, or it would have taught Hesiod and Pythagoras, as well as Xenophanes and Hecataeus."[69] In a note, Jones decries this criticism of Pythagoras in particular by saying of the fragment, "It is unfair to the mathematical achievements of Pythagoras . . . ."[70] To take offence, however, is to miss the point of what Heraclitus may be saying about *nous*. Here, the understanding is presented as that quality of mind allowing the human *ethos* to be carried into the *metaxy* as long as it is uncluttered with intellectual opinion-making, even when it's right. In other words,

---

69. Jones, XVI, p. 475.
70. Ibid.

we cannot rationally think our way to the divine ground any more than we can fly by flapping our arms. The higher Reason is that consciously developed quality of mind that recognizes the Logos when it hears it or perceives it in the world-order.

This important distinction between Reason and mere learning is expressed in another dubious fragment:

Pythagoras, son of Mnesarchus, practiced research more than any other man, and choosing out these writings claimed as his own a wisdom that was only much learning, a mischievous art.[71]

Here, research (*historia*) and another word for general learning (*polymathie*) make the point again that what passes for earthly wisdom is not spiritual wisdom. And as if this division formed a lasting part of the religious and philosophical life of the people of Ephesus, we have this passage from Paul's letter to the Ephesians, written some 600 years later:

Out of his infinite glory, may he give you the power through his Spirit for your hidden self to grow strong, so that Christ may live in your hearts through faith, and then, planted in love and built on love, you will with all the saints have the strength to grasp the breadth and the length, the height and the depth; until *knowing* the love of Christ, *which is beyond all knowledge*, you are filled with the utter fullness of god.[72] [author's emphasis]

In this passage the sense of "knowledge" is similar to grasping and relates to the same sense in Heraclitus of general learning and research. The "knowing" of the love of

---

71. Jones, XVII, p. 477.
72. *The Jerusalem Bible*, Ephesians, 3:14-21.

Christ to which Paul refers is that intuitive *gnosis* associated with mystical knowledge and has its grounding in the Heraclitean understanding (*nous*). When Anaxagoras took the word *nous* and made it limitless (part of the *apeiron* or infinite), one later result was the divinization of Mind, which in the Athenian high culture of the fifth century B.C.E. proved to be part of its arrogant downfall.[73] The clearest example of this divinization of Mind is played out by the tragic poet Sophocles, whose *Oedipus The King* was produced sometime around 430 or 429 B.C. at the height of Athenian power and influence. Sophocles' play is partly a warning to the Athenians to beware of the excesses of cleverness, of relying too much on the power of the cursive mind and the arrogance which comes with it in seeking out the truth.

Oedipus is the chief example of the man who depends to excess on the rational mind to solve personal and social problems and to exercise intellectual control over events. Seeking blindly to solve the crime of which he is unknowingly the guilty party, Oedipus is blind in his insight, has eyes but cannot see. His spiritual mirror, the blind seer Tieresias, tells Oedipus directly who he is and what his fate will be. Still, the clever Oedipus will not, cannot, see the truth until the evidence of his unholy crimes pile up and stare him in the face in the form of witnesses to his crimes. It is one of the great lessons of the play that the blind Tieresias is able to peer into the *metaxy* to understand and explicate true cause and effect.

This tendency to divinize human intellect was tempered by Plotinus, who, as we noted above, placed human consciousness in a continuous hierarchy at a higher point of

---

73. The best example of this fact is the famous Melian debate in Thucydides' account of the Peloponnesian War. An Athenian force lands on the island of Melos and demands surrender of its populace. The argument from the Athenians is that "might makes right," a bald display of arrogance which signaled the effective end of Athenian moral leadership in the Aegean.

which is the capacity, seldom realized, to merge with the *metaxy*. The cursive mind, or intellect, remains below this point and is subject to the vicissitudes of nature within which it dwells and with which it is fed. To this day philosophers and scientists debate the nature of this consciousness, with the latest round going to science, at least in the academic world.[74] At least the debate has narrowed its focus somewhat and is now attending to the transitional elements of mind where biology itself seems to have its basis at the quantum level. Eventually, it may be the province of quantum mechanics to explore the nature of higher consciousness. Philosophy, having rejected metaphysics, has given up the task.

In this present atmosphere of biology-based theories of consciousness, the fragments of Heraclitus encourage us to maintain some thoughtful distance from reductive definitions of human *ethos*. Although the fragments are certainly ruins of an archaic temple looming out of the marshes of the Ephesian landscape of Asia Minor, they nonetheless capture for us the genius and power of those visionaries who went before and who were unencumbered by pervasive attention to purely sense-based learning. Although fragmentary, the temple of Heraclitus nonetheless displays enough of colossal columns and delicate sculpture to affirm the builder's right to respect and admiration. Have we done as well in our constructs after 2,500 years? Where are our monuments to the *metaxy*, the "realm of the spiritual"? Will we pass along to the next era anything of similar worth?

---

74. At this writing, the newest offering is Paul Churchland's *The Engine of Reason, The seat of the Soul*, M.I.T. Press, Cambridge, 1995.

EPILOGUE

Toward a Heraclitean Theory of Consciousness

Emerging from the ideas expressed in *Logos, Physis, Nomos, Ethos and Telos* is a theory of human and divine consciousness which we may call Heraclitean. What suggests itself is the existence in the human *ethos* of a continuum of mental conditions — sleep, wakefulness, perception and self-consciousness — leading to the higher plane of the *metaxy* or "realm of the spiritual."[75] Such a continuum provides a basis for being-in-the-world as well as being-in-the-*apeiron* or, if you will, consciousness of the Infinite. Fragment 7 reminds us, **The way up and the way down are one and the same.** This metaphysical statement — for surely it is one — is not only a resolution of opposites, but is also designed to shatter our sensory perceptions of good and evil, pleasure and pain, life and death, and to realize this continuum of experience, both in the world and in the *apeiron*.

Aurobindo is helpful at this point. On the subject of Fragment 7, he says,

> The distinction of Heraclitus among the early Greek sages is his conception of the upward and downward road, one and the same in the descent and the return. It corresponds to the Indian idea of *nivrtti* and *pravrtti,* the double movement of the Soul and Nature .... The Indian sages were preoccupied with this double principle so far as it touches the action of the

---

75. Actually, a full continuum would also be expressed by conditions or altered states such as coma, deep sleep, dreaming, sleepwalking, hypnogogic states, waking sleep, awareness, self-consciousness, heightened awareness, meditational states, enlightened states, Nirvana.

individual soul entering into the procession of Nature
and drawing back from it.[76]

This reference to the transmigration of the soul expresses
the sense of noetic movement from the human to the divine
and back again, a movement reflective of a more Western
understanding of revelation found in traditional Judeo-
Christian texts.

The fragments also call for contemporary theorists or
philosophers of consciousness to revitalize metaphysical
thought on noetic grounds more relevant to a more radical
knowledge and awareness. As Eric Voegelin explains in
Anamnesis, the philosophical investigation of noesis is of
vital importance in understanding human *ethos*. Historically,
it was Thomas Aquinas who ignored classical noesis and
destroyed metaphysics by treating transcendent knowledge
as a collection of principles, universals and substances. Thus
exposed to the scientific knife, what Voegelin calls "noetic
exegesis" was surgically, even rather gleefully, removed from
philosophy by Voltaire.[77] Voegelin clarifies his point:

For when noesis is put into the same basket as "metaphysics," we lose the reality of knowledge of the
noetic experience and also the differentiated experience of the *ratio*, which means that we have no noetic
science of order any more.[78]

Currently, the emerging field of noetic science is attempting to relocate into the techniques of our own time and sci-

76. Sri Aurobindo, p. 23.
77. Eric Voegelin, *Anamnesis*, p. 193. Classical Noesis is best described as
the structure of the *Logos* in its relationship to human *ethos*. Noetic experience changes the way we perceive reality by "making transparent the material structure of consciousness (*ratio*).
78. Ibid, p. 194.

entific methodology a means of defining a more expansive range of human perception into phenomena not immediately perceived by the senses. The result of this research may well result in giving up a term like transcendent in favor of simply extending human sensory and intellectual perception into a broader, more transparent reality, even through the superficialities of the so-called paranormal. If we insist on clinging to the past, we can still speak of different realms of reality, or we can take a real Leap of Being of our own and talk instead of a single expansive realm of reality. In fact, there is no *other* realm. Reality is here, but 'here' is a very great concept, or we might say, 'here' has many rooms or dimensions.

Why must we move from one so-called realm to another as if through discreet barriers when we can merely extend our perception into the greater space within which we find ourselves? It is convenient, of course, to speak of the sensory realm if what we mean by it is the perception possible with unaided senses, an area which is, however, totally arbitrary. New technology has seriously blurred the edges of that definition by providing us with tiny, electronically enhanced tools and huge mechanistic tools to extend sensory perception well beyond "natural" ranges in the micro-and-macrocosms.

If we wish, we can refer, for example, to "penetrating the veil" of reality rather than refer to the spiritual as in some way 'other.' What we have called the spiritual realm is off the scale of ordinary human perception (including its technical instruments) but nonetheless is thoroughly accessible to intuitive perception with the right noetic knowledge and understanding. Our technical instruments allow us right now to hear pitches higher than our normal auditory range and to see bands of light beyond our normal visual field. We may consider the "realm of the spiritual" as simply beyond even that extended range of perception, but still within our grasp at some point or, better yet, at some higher (or other) range of consciousness. Nature, then, encompasses one continuous realm with a much broader range of existence than we are able presently to perceive. In the fragments of Heraclitus we are presented with such an expansive set of perceptions. Indeed, the fragments successfully expand the range of ordinary perception.

The Matrix of Reality

In his book *The Examined Life,* the philosopher Robert Nozick explores the Greek concept of *telos* as part of what he calls a matrix of reality. The category of *telos* in his matrix contains values such as completeness, greatness, beauty, height (as in reaching beyond), creativity, individuality, and wholeness. These values are highly charged values in our emotional life. We find them loaded with cultural definitions of success: money, reputation, titles, and honors.

Nozick points out, however, that the matrix has another, higher, category, that of the ideal limit, with values such as perfection, omnipotence, holiness, infinitude, infinite energy, sui generis (being one of a kind, totally distinctive), and all-encompassing. We see in these values an expansion of the ordinary human condition, what in the past would have been considered the persona of a hero or god. We do not, most of us, aspire to the ideal limit, except in theory. *Telos,* however, is our birthright, the *telos* of our being.

For Heraclitus, *telos* is the natural movement toward and direction of the spiritual nature of human beings, the primary goal in this life being the acquisition of wisdom. : **To be wise is one thing: to know the thought that directs all things through all things** (Fragment 34). If all things are in flux, however, then the human being exists in a state of flux, of Becoming, perceiving events which in turn are in flux. As Voegelin realized, meaning (*telos*) must detach itself from the flux of space/time in order to be expressive of the Logos, or Being, which does not exist in space/time and yet which partakes in it. *Telos*, then, is that quality of consciousness existing in the *metaxy*, that still, fixed point of Being in expanded space/time between the Logos itself and the limited *ethos*; it is the transition from mortality to immortality. Thus, we can say the following of the terms used in this text:

The Logos is the eternal, conscious basis of the world order, the true home of the human soul, embodied and otherwise. *Physis* is change and flux, the ever-living fire bursting forth and going out in measure. *Ethos* expresses the essence of human nature: existing in space/time using the flux of existence to establish an order of the mind and of the soul. Its nature is such that it has the potential to partake of Being in its Becoming. *Telos* is the natural but rare movement into the *metaxy*, the in-between where *ethos* and Logos intersect in transition and transformation. It is a noetic state based on intuition and the objective presence of the eternally emanating Logos.

As we tried to "re-member" Heraclitus, we encountered the seeming danger of assembling a figure who resembles a modern man. In other words, in looking for Heraclitus we may have found ourselves looking in contemporary mirrors instead of through the window of history. Hopefully, looking for Heraclitus in his fragments was a task more like enlightened archaeology, that is, digging through dirt and rocks to mysterious layers of the past in order to make sense of the present. Given the history of Heraclitean scholarship, however, we are saved from some of the dangers of self-referencing observation by the extent of historical depth. The 2,300 years of philosophy of Plato through Voegelin and the scholarship of Hippocrates through Kirk and Raven keep the light focused on the original figure as much as such a thing is possible. What is legitimately reflective of present concerns and perceptions, however, is the timeless nature of the fragments themselves in their poetic suggestiveness. The fragments are still mirrors of the greater human *ethos* as well as being intimations of the divine Logos capable of reflecting rare ranges of light. Therefore, isn't it also right that Heraclitus himself — reflected in his fragments — is also timeless, as much the modern figure as the ancient one?

This last assumption — or question — reveals the author's personal conviction that human ethos has changed very little in five thousand years. I do not believe that advances in technology have advanced our understanding of the mysteries of existence beyond what the so-called ancients understood. In fact, technology may well have blurred our vision substantially. Those moderns who assume an arrogant superiority in the face of ancient culture reveal in that arrogance their own superficial knowledge. In the same way, those who bemoan the loss of esoteric knowledge in the ruins of the past have also lost faith in their own intuitive capabilities. Those who choose to escape the present in favor of sentimentalizing the past also waste the present moment by ignoring its code. Heraclitus shows us how to recover the past in our quest to understand the present.

Consciousness Theory

A history of modern consciousness theory from Descartes to the present is highlighted by both victories and defeats in the effort to define the nature of consciousness and how human beings either use or are used by it. Cartesian theory divides mind and body into distinct realms so that the mind/soul (*res cogitans*) is effectively removed from any identification with the decaying body.[79] Descartes nonetheless located this conscious soul within the pineal gland, an interesting suggestion

---

79. *res cogitans* for Descartes was the substance which constitutes mind and was the mind which thinks.

at the time in that no one knew the proper function of the pineal gland, and its location at the very center of the brain mass made it a good candidate for the physical seat of the insubstantial soul. Although the gland is still mysterious, we now have evidence that it is part of the endocrine system and may regulate the timing of hormone releases at appropriate stages of physical development.[80]

We now understand that it does no good to try to "locate" consciousness in any specific place in the body, even in the brain. As soon as a theorist locates consciousness in some specific place, the effect of the placement defines and limits the nature of consciousness to that location. The error of such a tendency lies in asking where consciousness resides, rather than properly asking, first, what consciousness is like, and then, if possible, describing the faculties which make it possible and give it definition.

In Fragments 14 and 15 Heraclitus steers us away from seeking out tangible locations for intangible things. He tells us that **A hidden connection is stronger than an apparent one,** and, **Nature prefers to hide.** Read as answers to specific questions about the nature and place of the Logos or the nature and place of consciousness, Heraclitus directs us away from "research" and instead tells us to describe carefully observed experience. If the Logos is all-pervasive, for example, then so too is consciousness. We define it by observing its most complex functions. In other words, we must be part of it rather than it being part of us.

Here is a theory: The central nervous system forms part of the highly sophisticated terminus for the reception of messages from the greater consciousness, that is, the intelligence at the heart of nature and the cosmos. The function of the brain is to attune these impulses into local coherence, thus

---

80. For example, a calcified pineal gland in a young male child accelerates the development of the sexual organs well beyond the normal range of growth.

helping to build formal structures in the mind with which we can understand and direct our lives. Consciousness, then, exists everywhere, and living systems, including human beings, transmit this consciousness in their unique, species-specific way, as do bees, ants, trees and algae.

Materialists insist that the brain is the one and only source of consciousness, which in the light of the theory above is the same as saying that the individual radio is the source of the program it plays. When we turn the radio off, the music it was playing is still "out there," although not in the same form as we hear it by virtue of the localizing instrument. The brain and its connective tissue works in the same way.

When Heraclitus refers to the Sibyl at Delphi, he does so in recognition of this function of consciousness within the human *ethos*. The human being, properly awake and prepared, becomes aware of consciousness beyond the mentality of the physical nervous system in its narrow range of functioning. Being awake, however, is his description of the state of awareness beyond the limited grasp of logic, even of "common" sense.

When we do not permit ourselves to reason beyond our tangible experience, we set limits on our conclusions. The skeptical David Hume (1711-1776), for example, narrowed the matter down this way:

> For my part, when I enter most intimately into what I call *myself*, I always stumble on some particular perception or other, of heat or cold, light or shade, love or hatred, pain or pleasure. I never can catch *myself* at any time without a perception, and never can observe any thing but the perception. When my perceptions are remov'd for any time, as by sound sleep, so long am I insensible of *myself*, and may truly be said not to exist. And were all my perceptions

remov'd by death, and cou'd I neither think, nor feel, nor see, nor love, nor hate, after the dissolution of my body, I shou'd be entirely annihilated, nor do I conceive what is farther requisite to make me a perfect non-entity. If any one upon serious and unprejudic'd reflexion, thinks he has a different notion of *himself*, I must confess I can reason no longer with him. All I can allow him is, that he may be in the right as well as I, and that we are essentially different in this particular. He may, perhaps, perceive something simple and continu'd, which he calls *himself*; tho' I am certain there is no such principle in me.[81]

Hume presents a logically argued statement that is not really concerned with an exploration into reality as much as it is with an insistence upon the limits of his own mental perceptions. In the passage, Hume consciously limits himself to being an expert in analyzing shadows on the wall of his own cave. In Heraclitus, on the other hand, we are constantly taken out of such limits of perception into greater possibility, not for the sake of satisfying images of heaven and eternal life, but for the sake of consciousness itself and to help us anticipate and imagine a fuller range of human *ethos*.

After Hume, Descartes, and the so-called Enlightenment, and after the Romantic reaction of the German Idealists, we entered the world of the materialists and scientific hegemony. All consideration of consciousness came under the scrutiny of scientific proof and the evidence of experimentation, that is, of technical observation and laboratory measurement. The young science of psychology took for itself the nature and ranges of human and animal behavior, describing, categorizing, cataloguing, and inescapably reducing conscious-

---

81. David Hume, *A Treatise of Human Nature (Body, Mind and Death*, ed. Anthony Flew. Collier Books, New York, 1964, p. 189.

ness to the limits of its own narrow definitions. The culmination of this reductionism was the effort of B. F. Skinner and his followers to expunge any mention of mind from the language of psychology and replace it with reactions to external stimulus and motor responses. Here was reductionism at its most extreme. Mind disappeared in favor of measurable brain activity.

Much of Skinner's work in the 1930s and 1940s was a reaction to the excesses of Freud's imaginative work on the human mind. Freud had succeeded in pushing science into the realm of the metaphoric and belittling the materialists' prosaic views of consciousness by imagining the hidden world of the unconscious in human *ethos*. Although hidden from rational observation, this activity was still seen as materially based. We cannot even call Freud's human motivations a *telos*, so limited are his survival and pleasure-oriented goals. The resulting reductionism in Freud's writings, although highly imaginative, together with the impact of Darwin's systematic evolutionary doctrines, had the effect of confining the mind once again to very narrow functioning. We were reduced to the level of rational animals in a universe where random events and biological motives dictated our genetically flawed condition. It was in that atmosphere that Skinner attempted to rid us of mentality altogether as a messy, unpredictable disturbance to society.

In the past fifty years, however, the fields of cognitive science, archetypal psychology, and a rebellion in philosophy from the cramped syntax of the logical positivists, has revitalized the barren, eroded landscape of *physis* and *ethos*. As we explore in greater depth the nature of the mind-body connection and the so-called mind-brain problem, we discover through new technology joined to more open theorizing about consciousness that we are less a biologically determined body with an eternal Mind and more of an inexhaustibly complex bundle of universe stuff capable of wide-ranging perception and potential. We are instruments of the Infinite: seers, explicators, definers, artists, planners, imaginers, instigators.

What Emerson called Universal Mind or Over-Soul has come to mean in this new paradigm the ever expanding environment of consciousness and intelligent planetary energy within which we take our life and exercise our individual existences. Almost in spite of itself, science shows us every day the sophistication of cellular existence, with its subtle communications, complex structures, and intelligent social organization. Heraclitus is correct when he affirms that we will never fathom the essential mysteries of the Logos. Ours is a different task, even as we exercise our natural curiosity. Fragment 39 opens for us the range of our inquiries: **You would not find out the boundaries of soul, even by traveling along every path, so deep a measure does it have.**

An example of the way in which science has been able to expand our perceptions of consciousness without a reductionist point of view is reflected in the work of people like Roger Penrose, whose mathematical, biological, quantum anti-computational approach to consciousness offers new revelations that contribute to our quest for knowledge.[82] What Penrose has done, along with other adventurers like him who explore the wilderness of consciousness, is to begin a coherent discussion of consciousness and mind theory on the assumption that we are looking at a profoundly wide and deep range of experience which is only partially reflected in measurable mechanisms.

Part of what Penrose has done focuses attention on the microtubules of the cellular cytoskeleton, where, he suggests, the fundamental elements of the greater consciousness may form into recognizable human mental life in the quantum

---

82. Roger Penrose, *Shadows of the Mind,* Oxford University Press, Oxford, 1994. See Chapter entitled "Quantum Theory and the Brain."

movements and rhythms of subatomic particles. The micro-tubules contained in all our body cells may be the means by which consciousness gathers itself into coherent form in the brain to make thinking possible.

Quantum activity is chaotic and is, therefore, measured statistically. At the quantum level we speak of probabilities rather than mathematical laws. Whether or not Penrose's microtubules are crucial to the process or not, quantum activity at some point shifts into the Newtonian classical physics of time and space. This process must occur in obedience to natural law or in Heraclitus' world, the Logos manifesting in nature. Quanta thus become lawfully "arranged" out of chaos, recapitulating the formation of the cosmos itself in each moment. In this sense, we are indeed, each of us, a fiery universe in formation, bursting forth and going out in measure. We can also rightly say that we are attuned to the whole, using the Greek word *harmonia*. The attunement creates the structures which eventually become atoms, molecules, proteins, and eventually, DNA. The rest is history, literally. It is in this way that DNA measures the human situation within which we frame our existence. All is One.

A principle: Human beings possess eyes because a cosmic phenomenon we call light exists. We have ears because vibrations causing sound exist. We have noses because molecules capable of producing odor exist.[83] If we wish to study light, then, we study the eye, which light created. We study the ear to know the nature of sound and the nose to know the nature of odors. When Heraclitus said that he searched for himself, he knew that to know the cosmos he must know himself because he was an exact microcosm of that cosmos.

In the same way, we are conscious creatures because consciousness "out there" in nature exists, and it exists indepen-

---

83. Aristotle had Heraclitus saying, "If all existing things were to become smoke, the nostrils would distinguish them." (Jones, XXXVII, p. 483).

dent of and external to human mental life. We are conscious because consciousness exists, and we can study the greater consciousness by knowing human consciousness. What we and other creatures did, along with developing eyes, ears and noses, was to absorb from the Logos the fundamental characteristics and mechanisms of consciousness so as to develop organs of mental perception in order to know in just the same way as light created the eye. What we are also doing, and have been doing from the beginning, is to continue this emanation from the Logos in order to expand our mental environment as needed. Human personal and collective longing for something beyond the physical universe is the mechanism of the a priori knowledge through which the world of consciousness enters our *ethos*.

Conclusion

Heraclitus left us fragments of a life-long teaching in the form of observations and instigations directed toward creating a conscious, self-examined life. His purpose was to illuminate an awareness of the Logos, that conscious and pervasive power which has as a manifestation of itself the universe we increasingly know and desire to understand. His method of instigation was to rise above the moribund mythological language and poetic expression of his time to turn his students away from the banal and to shock them into realizations of universal law.

Knowing that human beings are caught in body-mind duality, Heraclitus first breaks down the easy oppositions of sensory perception and yet also establishes the necessity of opposing tension as the means by which the Logos creates and sustains the universe in unity. When he states that strife is necessary, he shows how it serves us well when we understand how the back-bending tension and release inherent in the bow, the lyre, and life itself give birth to new forms and are able to penetrate the opaque layers of habit built up by deadening sleep.

It may be possible to experience something of the transforming effect of Heraclitus' language if we allow some of the fragmentary images or phrases free rein in our minds, to flow together without conscious dedication to cursive syntax. For example:

> . . . follow the universal . . . agree that all things are one . . . one and the same . . . out of all things . . . a unity . . . all things are beautiful and good and just . . . an unapparent connection . . . expect the unexpected . . . strife is universal . . . all things happen through conflict . . . the father of all . . . it divides, gathers . . . all things in process . . . all things in motion . . . directs all things . . . thought directs all things . . . dry soul is best . . . so deep a measure . . . living their death and dying their life . . . searched myself . . . the logos is one.

These are the essentials, these and as well the challenging ideas that arise from close analysis of whole thoughts. What is startling in the final analysis is the lack of what we might call discussion or argument in the fragments. Heraclitus does not, except possibly in Fragment 1, pose problems the way Plato does or investigate a topic the way Aristotle does for the simple reason that he lifts us above cursive explanations into the rarified ether in which the gods breathe the Logos.

In sum, in 500 B.C., during an era when Being in the form of text entered human consciousness, into the ordinary, myth-drenched way in which we were seeing the world, stepped Heraclitus, set apart from his past and his birth-directed destiny, focusing the attention of interested followers away from the ordinary and onto the objects of their deepest instincts. As they began to see in a new way, mistaken observations were turned inward, torn away from the fabric of habitual thinking, and cast aside. Deeper perceptions took their place and were tested in a whole new consciously fired landscape. Heraclitus pointed the way without saying "Follow me;" instead, he served as the bow releasing the arrow of exploration into the vibrant air. In that sense he was the first true philosopher, not intending to create a religion, found a school, establish a way of life, or even begin a debate. Like Socrates, he saw himself as the gadfly of his culture, but he was also more. He was a lover of the truth, and like all true lovers, he cared more for the truth than he did for himself.

Human beings may take an active part, if they will, in the Logos of the universe, insofar as they participate through insight in the consciousness which is our connection to the Logos. Our *ethos* is capable of comprehending the Logos as revelation through the developed powers of intuition. An accumulation of such revelation put to use is called wisdom. Often, human arrogance (*hybris*) seeks a private understanding or personal possession of insight, resulting in a closing down of this intuitive power. The result is dogmatism and ideology.

The more that human beings openly and humbly seek higher knowledge, the more they develop the power to perceive it, until finally they penetrate to the hidden universal order. The result of this penetration is knowledge of the Logos, that which "directs all things through all things." The acquisition of this knowledge is not an event; it is a stance in the world. It is Being in its fullness.

Appendix

The Problem of the Text

The first challenge in reading Heraclitus is finding his text, what is left of it. The assumption has always been that there was a "book," actually a scroll, probably called "On Nature," if it had a title, which contained the aphoristic materials attributed to Heraclitus. No evidence exists beyond vague references from much later philosophers that such a scroll existed. Some commentators — like Sri Aurobindo, for example — simply ignore the fragmentary nature of the text and write as if what remains is intellectually or systematically complete. Others of a more cautionary nature are reluctant to draw any conclusions at all in the light of such thin content. Between those extremes lies the responsible approach, namely, to acquire some understanding of the sources behind the fragments.

The number and intellectual quality of the ancient commentators who quote Heraclitus to their own ends, a list which includes Hippocrates, Plato and Aristotle, to name the three most notable, and the number of scholars and commentators who have examined the slim remains, tends strongly toward the conclusion that Heraclitus did indeed write down in aphoristic prose an extended formal composition, excerpts from which make up the extant corpus. To what end he wrote, however, is more problematic. If, as we suppose, Heraclitus was a teacher to a select group (*aristoi* of the mind) of pupils, then the sayings might have been collected for their benefit to summarize the master's essential philosophical position. More of that below.

The same would have been the case with the great teachers of that and earlier time. Of the great teachers of the sixth century B.C. we have little or no material written in their own words. All of the sayings of the Buddha, Zoroaster,

Pythagoras and Jeremiah (probably written down by Baruch or even later scholars), follow their active ministries by some years. For Confucius and Lao-Tse, however, the tradition is that the works we have are from their own hands. In all of these cases, however, the oral tradition was the dominant mode of instruction.

In the case of Heraclitus, all of the fragments are quoted in the works of others, and of these only a limited number are direct quotations. The reason we can be so certain that the phrasing of the fragments can be attributed to Heraclitus has to do with their unique style. His ambiguity, humor, irony, and heresies stamp the sayings with an indelible sound and sense. What is less clear, however, and what we would like to know, is what overall form the sayings took, whether in book form similar to *Proverbs*, or as a collection of koans for daily meditation, or, less likely, a gospel account written down later by devoted adherents.

The one important clue is provided by Sextus Empiricus, the third century A.D. physician and philosopher. When Sextus quotes the great first fragment, the longest we have, and then "a little further on he adds" Fragment 2, we sense the existence of a prose text containing an argument. If the text was a collection of aphorisms, Sextus might have said, "In another place," or "in another saying." With this kind of slim evidence, we have concluded that what we have remaining to us are fragments from a single book, and not a loose collection of aphorisms or the collected remembrances of his pupils, although the latter is still very possible.

For the purposes of this examination of these fragments, we have decided to concentrate on those which form complete thoughts as the springboard to our own text. There is in a complete sentence enough of an arc of a circle to invite closure in an expanded paragraph. It is with that conviction that these expanded commentaries do not follow the usual example of scholars who examine and dispute among themselves as to what, exactly, Heraclitus might have meant in phrases or in single words.

The Problem of Order

The placing of the fragments in an order happens naturally in the mind, which has a natural tendency to classify and to bring what appears to be random in experience into a comfortable design. The fragments of Heraclitus have been collected very much as if they were picked up from the ground after having fallen out of an airplane. They come down to us in no order that allows for any obvious sequential interpretation, except in those few cases such as when Sextus Empiricus indicates a sequence. In these cases most editors have followed those small leads.

Since any editorial order is essentially arbitrary, it depends on the commentator's idea of order to assert itself. Where one edition arranges the fragments loosely by subject, namely fragments on the universe (really the whole collection), on politics and ethics, and on religion, another follows an alphabetical order of the ancient sources. Kirk arranges them by subject, as he says, for clarity and convenience and warns others that to attempt a canonical order is "foredoomed to failure." His groupings have the positive value of helping the reader to grasp the more abstract terms such as Logos and then to move to more practical or concrete fragments based on these abstractions. A. H. Robinson arranged the fragments by alphabetical listing of commentator, except for Fragments 1 and 2, which clearly appear early.

The design of the present text has been to see the fragments as the remnants of a lifetime of teaching. It is a principle of sound instruction that the teacher begins at the present level of understanding of his pupils and then moves by steps to the desired goal. This principle suggests that if the remains of the work of Heraclitus are indeed fragments from a book intended as a guide to others to reach an understanding of reality, then to choose a sequence that forms a logical sequence of instruction might be a valid approach. I have followed that approach.

The Problem of Purpose

If the book attributed to Heraclitus constitutes a teaching, that would mean it is not a traditional religious or revelatory document. It is not, in other words, a cosmology similar to the *Theogony* of Hesiod, nor is it a Homeric Hymn like *The Earth Mother*, even though Heraclitus is often included in this cosmological company. It seems clear, in fact, that Heraclitus is aiming in his apophatic way at contradicting most of the religious and mythical dogma of Hellenic tradition. It is doubtful, then, that his book would take the same form as the dogma he wished to erase from the minds of his pupils.

To erase a received tradition requires of a good teacher the obligation to replace in the subsequent void something of value. Heraclitus was not a nihilist. What he had discovered through the discipline of self-inquiry (**I searched my nature.**) was that an individual could achieve a level of wisdom (*to sophon*) that would penetrate the illusions and opinions (*doxa*) to some beneficial end, that end comprising a knowledge of Being. The commentators were perfectly willing to state *their* ends, and these personal opinions are sometimes attributed to Heraclitus. One spurious fragment, for example, says, "It is the concern of all human beings to know themselves and to be serious-minded." Another is "To be serious-minded is the greatest virtue, and wisdom is to speak the truth and to act it, listening to the voice of nature." There is little in these aphorisms that sound like Heraclitus, but that others might attribute such thoughts to him is natural enough.

As to assigning authenticity and grouping, then, I have elected to follow somewhat the current standard in the area of Heraclitus studies: *The Presocratic Philosophers*, G .S. Kirk, J. E. Raven and M. Schofield, a text commonly referred to simply as "Kirk and Raven." Their selection and numbering, because Heraclitus follows others in their text, commences with 194. For simplicity, I have renumbered to begin with 1 and deviated somewhat into my own order according to commentary in the text. Also, I have included a few more fragments than are referred to in Kirk and Raven, but generally I follow their division of authentic and dubious. Those interested in examining all the fragments, both certain and dubious, should refer to volume four of *Hippocrates* (which includes the fragments of Heraclitus) translated by W. H. S. Jones; Harvard University Press, Cambridge.

THE ESSENTIAL FRAGMENTS

1. The Logos, which is as I describe, proves incomprehensible, both before it is heard and even after it is heard. For although all things happen according to the Logos, many act as if they have no experience of it, even when they do experience such words and action as I explain, as when I separate out each thing according to its nature and state how it is; but as to the rest, they fail to notice what they do after they wake up, just as they forget what they do when they sleep.

2. It is necessary, therefore, to obey the universal; but although the Logos is universal, most people act as though they had a private understanding.

3. Listening to the Logos and not to me, it is wise to agree that all things are One.

4. I prefer the things which yield to seeing, hearing and thus to perception.

5. Eyes and ears are bad witnesses, especially if we have souls that do not understand their language.

6. When they are spoken to, the ignorant are like the deaf: they bear witness to the proverb that when present they are absent.

7. The way up and the way down are one and the same.

8. Of all the accounts I have heard, not one rises to this: to know that wisdom is separate from all things.

9. We have as One in us that which is living and dead, waking and sleeping, young and old: because these having transformed are those, and those having transformed are these.

10. Everything taken together is whole but also not whole, what is being brought together and taken apart, what is in tune and out of tune; out of diversity there comes unity, and out of unity diversity.

11. God is day/night, winter/summer, war/peace, fullness/hunger; the experience of God changes in the way that [wine], when it is mixed with spices, is named according to the scent of each.

12. Human nature does not have true judgment, but divine nature does.

13. To God all things are beautiful, good and just, but human beings have supposed some things to be unjust, others just.

14. A hidden connection is stronger than an apparent one.

15. Nature prefers to hide.

16. They do not apprehend how being in conflict it still agrees with itself; there is an opposing coherence, as in the tensions of the bow and lyre.

17. If we do not expect the unexpected we will not discover it, since it is not to be searched out and is difficult to apprehend.

18. It is necessary to know that conflict is universal and that strife is right, and that all things happen through strife and necessity.

19. Strife is the father of All That Is and king of All That Is, and some participants he shows as immortal, others as mortal; some he makes slaves, others free.

20. Good and bad are the same.

21. New and different waters flow around those who step into the same river. It disperses and comes together . . . flows in and out . . . towards us and away.

22. [Heraclitus says somewhere that] . . . all things are in process and nothing stays still, and [comparing all things to flowing waters, he says] we cannot step twice in the same river.

23. Over-weaning pride is the sacred disease (as opposed to epilepsy).

24. This cosmos [the unity of all that is] was not made by immortal or mortal beings, but always was, is and will be an eternal fire, arising and subsiding in measure.

25. Fire's alternations: first as sea, and of sea half earth and half lightning dispersed as sea, and measured in the same proportion as existed before it became earth.

26. All things equally exchange for fire as does fire for all things, as goods are exchanged for gold and gold for goods.

27. The lightning directs everything.

30. What we call "hot" seems to be immortal and to apprehend all things: to see and hear and know all things, both present and future. This otherness, then, the diversity of the all, when things become clouded, went out to the furthermost revolution, and seems to me to have been what was called ether by the men of old.

31. It makes more sense to throw out a corpse than manure.

32. The sun is new each day.

33. If the Sun transgresses his proper measure, the Furies will find him out.

34. To be wise is one thing: to know the thought that directs all things through all things.

35. The One, the only wisdom, does and yet does not consent to be called Zeus.

36. It is death for souls to become water, as it is death for water to become earth; water comes to be from earth, as soul comes from water.

37. A dry soul is wisest and best.

38. When he is drunk, thus having his soul moist, a man is led about by an immature boy, stumbling and not knowing where he is going.

39. You would not find out the limits of the soul, even by traveling along every path, so deep a logos does it have.

40. At night man kindles a light for himself when his eyes fail to see; thus in life, he is in contact with the dead when asleep and with the sleeper when awake.

41. [According to Heraclitus] we acquire understanding by drawing in the Logos through breathing, as we are forgetful when asleep, we regain our senses when we wake up again. For in sleep, when the channels of perception are shut, our mind is shaken loose from its surroundings, and breathing is the only point of contact, to hold on rather like a root; being separated then, our mind loses its former power of memory. But in the waking state it again looks out through the channels of perception as through a kind of window, and meeting with the surroundings it puts on the power of Reason.

42. Do not act and speak as if asleep.

43. In its presence, [the Logos?] they rise up and become conscious guardians of the living and dead.

44. Dogs bark at strangers.

45. Human beings are carried away by every new theory.

46. Immortal mortals, mortal immortals, living their death and dying their life.

47. It is better to keep ignorance hidden.

48. They purify themselves in vain of blood-guilt by defiling themselves with blood, as though one who had stepped into mud were to wash with mud; he would appear insane if anyone noticed him doing this. Further, they pray to statues

as if one were to carry on a conversation with houses, not recognizing the true nature of gods and spirits.

49. We should not act like the children of our parents

50. Those who sleep also share in the work of the cosmos.

51. The divine one whose oracle is in Delphi speaks neither directly or obscurely, but rather gives a sign.

52. The raving Sibyl, through the god, utters somber, unembellished, unperfumed sayings, reaching over a thousand years with her voice.

53. I searched my nature.

54. For human beings, character is the divine force.

55. Hesiod is the teacher of the Many, but he did not understand that day and night are One.

56. It is better for men that they not obtain all they wish.

57. Those who speak with sense rely on what is universal, as a city must rely on its law, and with much greater reliance. For all human laws are nourished by one divine law; for it has as much power as it wishes and is sufficient for all with more left over.

Glossary of Greek Terms

apeiron: Beyond; the Indefinite; the infinite, Eternal
apophasis: denial, negation
daimon   spirit, minor god, destiny
ethos: character, essence of human nature
gnosis: intuitive knowing
hybris: arrogance, over-weaning pride
logos: word, account, cosmic law, Absolute
metaxy: in between, place between, gap
nomoi: the laws, customs, cultural norms
nous: mind, consciousness, sometimes soul
psyche: soul or self
physis: nature, natural law, sometimes natural
                human inclination
polis: city-state, community
ta panta: all things, everything, the cosmos, diversity
telos: end, purpose, meaning, also directed end

SUGGESTED READING

Those interested in pursuing Heraclitus further might find the following books informative. They represent a wide spectrum of Heraclitus studies.

―――― Heracleitus. *Hippocrates,* vol. IV. (W.H.S. Jones, trans. Harvard University Press, Cambridge, 1931). This volume from the Loeb series is the standard Greek text and translation of all the fragments, certain and dubious.

Heidegger, Martin and Fink, Eugen. *Heraclitus Seminar* (Northwestern University Press, Evanston, IL., 1970). A challenging examination of Greek terms appearing in the fragments. Of particular interest is Heidegger's interest in *ta panta,* "all things."

Kirk, G.S., Raven, J.E., Schofield, M., *The Presocratic Philosophers* (Cambridge University Press, Cambridge, 2nd edition, 1983). The standard text for anyone interested in the Presocratics. Contains the Greek texts, translation and extensive commentary.

Robinson, T.M. *Heraclitus* (University of Toronto Press, Toronto, 1987). A reliable text with excellent source material. Well organized and clear.

Sri Aurobindo, *Heraclitus* (Sri Aurobindo Ashram, Pondicherry, India, 1941). An excellent essay on the philosophy of Heraclitus from one of the best minds of the twentieth century. The pamphlet is available from the Matagiri Aurobinbdo Center, 218 Wittenberg Rd., Mt. Tremper, NY 12457. email: Matagiri@aol.com